Grammar Saves Lives!

Professional Writing for Law Enforcement Officers

By Steven Starklight

Copyright 2012 Steven Starklight

AND

Grammar Saves Lives!
Volume 2

Professional Writing for Law Enforcement Officers

By Steven Starklight

Copyright 2020 Steven Starklight

THE COMPLETE SET

Volume 1 Table of Contents

Author's Preface:

I wrote this book about eight years ago. A lot has happened in eight years. A lot has changed in our profession. In fact, it's almost unrecognizable to the state of policing when I started in 1993. Luckily, a few things have not changed, and one of them is the need for cops to write properly. That will never change.

There are a lot of books out there that are geared to law enforcement officers (LEOs) and report writing. Most of them are a lot longer and more comprehensive than mine, and that's ok. My book won't be able to turn you into Mark Twain overnight- or ever.

I assume the majority of you already know the basics. The goal of my book is to show you some of the most common mistakes that I see LEOs make in their writing, and give you the tools you need to avoid making those mistakes, and to write a more bulletproof report.

Since 2012, I've had some time to think about this book, and whether it's sufficient. With COVID-19, I've had a lot more time to think, and to write. That extra free time helped me write and perfect Volume 2, which came out in August 2020, and now you can buy both volumes as a single set and save even more money.

I wish you all the best in your pursuit of law, order, and justice.

Steven Starklight

August 2020

Introduction:

How many times have you found yourself sitting in a chair looking down at your incident report, dripping with red ink, wondering where you went wrong? Maybe you have sat in some lawyer's office on the receiving end of some verbal criticism about something you wrote, or failed to write, in a report. I specifically remember being in such a situation, listening to the assistant district attorney drone on, pontificating about all the ways my report would create problems at trial. I also remember imagining how that prosecutor would do in a uniform with a gun and badge dealing with the public and their problems.

There will always be someone willing to criticize everything you do. Just about everyone is an armchair critic of police procedure. It reminds me of a famous quote from Theodore Roosevelt, one that I had posted in my office when I was a police legal advisor to remind me where I stood in that agency. In fact, it embodies most of the reasons why I left the practice of law to return to law enforcement:

It is not the critic who counts: not the man who points out how the strong man stumbles or where the doer of deeds could have done better. The credit belongs to the man who is actually in the arena, whose face is marred by dust and sweat and blood, who strives valiantly, who errs and comes up short again and again, because there is no effort without error or shortcoming, but who knows the great enthusiasms, the great devotions, who spends himself for a worthy cause; who, at the best, knows, in the end, the triumph of high achievement, and who, at the worst, if he fails, at least he fails while daring greatly, so that his place shall never be with those cold and timid souls who knew neither victory nor defeat.

He is talking about you. He is talking about our police officers, our soldiers, those that devote their lives and their energy on "worthy causes." The role of the prosecutor (in criticizing your work), the role of police management, those in administrative roles, are all important, but it is the work you do on the street that makes the difference. Remember that.

You will see several quotes from President Roosevelt in this book, not because of some particular affinity he had for the police, or because he is my hero, but simply because he made some great statements that are quite relevant to our discussion.

Those of you with an astute eye are probably wondering why I would use a quote in a book on critical writing that minimizes the role of the critic and places the emphasis on one's deeds, not another's critique of those deeds. Well, first, it is a great quote!

Second, police officers fit perfectly in the role of the man in the arena. Prosecutors, supervisors, defense lawyers, citizens watching your every move, all these people will be critics of your work, all these cold, timid souls. The most important aspect of your job is in the field, but if you cannot properly document that work, then you will have problems. Your work in the arena will put a criminal behind bars; your written word is what will keep him there. That is why I use this quote. You must be a good LEO, but you must also be a good report writer. It really is that simple.

Police officers do not graduate from the academy and instantly know how to be critical thinkers and logical and technical writers. It takes a lot of practice. How often have you written a report and then, later, found yourself regretting something you wrote, or racking your brain trying to remember some relevant detail that you neglected to add? Are you frequently defending your writing as your supervisor or prosecutor picks it apart? Are you sick of it? You must be, because you bought this book, and I am going to make it worth every penny.

As a superior court judge once told me in the middle of a trial, "Counselor, the Devil is in the details!" He was right, so let's explore those details. Police officers are in a unique position in society. You must be fearless as a front line soldier, intelligent as a nuclear physicist, strong as an ox, and precise as a surgeon. You must not only have the requisite mental stamina and ability but the physical prowess to back it up. I defy you to identify a job with as much responsibility and as broad a set of conditions precedent as that of a beat cop.

And, as my lieutenant used to tell us at our squad meetings, nobody has more authority, more power, than a uniformed patrolman. To wield so much power, to have the brains and the brawn and the courage, to be able to balance all those characteristics makes for quite an individual. Unfortunately, it isn't enough. You must also be able to accurately document and describe your actions. That is where I come in. Your written work should be the mirror image, or reflection, of your work.

I cannot give you everything you need to be a successful police officer. That takes years and a lot of preparation and even a little luck. (If you are trying to break into the career, then I will insert a shameless plug for my other book, *How to Become a Police Officer: The Best Tactics to Get Police Officer Jobs and enter the Police Academy*.) This book is designed simply to address one aspect of what I believe is the most difficult (and rewarding) job in the country. The work police officers do is only as good as a police officer's ability to document it. Do not take this part of your job lightly.

This is not intended to be a back to basics guide to proper grammar, sentence construction and diagramming and all that high school stuff. There are plenty of much larger (and more expensive) books that cover those elementary rules and principles. This book presumes that you already know the difference between subject and verb, adjective and adverb. However, there are some basic rules and common mistakes with which you must be familiar when writing professionally, and I will make sure you understand them by the end of this book.

A word about the title: yes, it is catchy, and yes, the title was intended to draw people in and read my book. However, I firmly believe it is true. Grammar is one aspect of precision writing, along with punctuation, spelling, and content. Some of you are probably rolling your eyes, dismissing the priority I am placing on these topics. Let's look at a few examples. Here is an easy one: a man goes on a business trip for a few days. While he is away, he unwittingly sends the following text message to his wife:

Hi, having a great time in Vegas. Wish you were her.

I would guess the problem is fairly obvious. Proofread your work. When you finish proofreading it, put it down, walk away, then return and proofread it again. I just cannot emphasize that strongly enough.

If you do not pay attention to your writing, you could make as dangerous a mistake as our man on the business trip to Vegas.

Here's another great example, blatantly stolen from various blogs and websites on the Internet under the heading "Punctuation Saves Lives:"

Let's eat, Grandma!
Let's eat Grandma!

If the above requires explanation, your problems are way beyond my abilities. A comma is all that separates you from a happy day with family and life in prison!

By the way, take a closer look at this book: it is short and sweet. It is not a 300 page textbook with practical exercises and an examination at the end. It is not designed to be a college textbook. It is a down and dirty guide to professional writing for law enforcement officers. (By the way, for the rest of this book I will abbreviate law enforcement officer to LEO.) If you need special help on grammar, syntax, spelling and the like, get a book devoted to such things. I will give you some good ideas later in the book as to a few things that you should keep on your shelf when you are writing. As for you, my reader, this is a book written by a cop, for cops, about stuff that cops write about; nothing more, nothing less!

Now back to reality. Let's briefly discuss the necessity for precision in your writing. Compare, if you will, the following two excerpts taken from the same single (and imaginary) witness statement:

Frank told me that he told him Jones killed her, but not her friend. Frank said he last saw Jones at the corner of Fifth and Pine walking away from him holding a gun. Frank said that as he walked past that intersection he encountered Louise, and heard her tell him that Megan called him a jerk. Frank heard him tell her that he would kill her and that she was a bitch.

Frank said that Jones told Frank that Jones killed Jane, but not Megan. Frank said that he last saw Jones at the corner of Fifth and Pine walking south and holding a gun. Frank said that as Jones walked past that intersection he encountered Louise, and Frank heard Louise tell Jones that Megan called him a jerk. Frank heard

Jones tell Louise that he would kill Megan and that Megan was a bitch.

Reading the first statement, do you have a clue what Frank said? I certainly don't! Without precision and attribution (to be discussed shortly), your reports will have no value. In fact, they can actually provide *negative value.*

WAR STORY:

I was at an intersection in my car when someone threatened me with a gun. He was the passenger in a car that pulled up next to my car at the intersection. The passenger got out of his car, brandished a firearm, and threatened me. Just as I reached for my own weapon, another car pulled up between us in the empty third lane, and the attacker drove away. I called 911. A law enforcement officer (LEO) was dispatched to me to take my report and my statement. For whatever reason, this officer did not seem very interested in what I had to say. In fact, he was openly hostile.

The suspect was eventually arrested and the case went to trial. While meeting with the prosecutor, he provided me a copy of the LEO's initial incident report, which I had never read. I was shocked. I had provided the LEO exact quotes of the threat the suspect yelled, and an exact description of him, his vehicle, and even the weapon the suspect brandished. The LEO completely misquoted me, laid out the entire event incorrectly, and glossed over much of the detail I had provided. In short: he was a terrible writer.

On the day of trial, I spent two hours under cross examination. The defense attorney's weapon of choice was that LEO's initial report! Because of that officer's mistakes and indifference to the facts, not to mention his poor writing skills, we almost lost our case. His version of the facts was so warped that it made one of us look like a liar, and I promise you, I was telling the truth!

The war story I just told you is absolutely true, and one of several I will weave into the book if I think it is illustrative of a point I am trying to make. These are each true stories taken from my experience as a police officer or prosecutor or in one of my other law enforcement careers.

By the way, because I mentioned my experience, let me give you my quick resume. Perhaps you sought out this book after reading one of my others, like *Get a Gun and Badge Today* or *True Police Stories*. Then again, you might be reading this book because it was assigned to you at the police academy. Regardless of how you came across it, let me establish why I know what I am writing about: I have twenty years in the business, including time I spent as a prosecutor and as the legal advisor for a very large agency on the east coast. I started out as a uniform patrolman with a county police department, and have served over the years as a campus police officer, a district attorney's investigator, a deputy sheriff and for the last ten years as a special agent of the FBI. I have a degree in English, a Masters degree and a Juris Doctor (law degree). These were all studies that required a lot of professional, academic writing. I had to become a master of the *MLA*, the *Bluebook* and the *Elements of Style*.

I have been a prolific writer since I was a child, and still love to write, whether fiction or reference. I will tell you with no hesitation that what made my career so rewarding, so successful, has been my ability to write. I am good, but nothing special when it comes to shooting, to working cases, to physical agility or defensive tactics. However, I can write, and whether you believe it or not, writing is one skill that you cannot fake, and for which you cannot compensate in other ways. Just like your firearms instructors tell you about shooting, writing is a learned skill, and the concept of "muscle memory" applies with equal strength to writing. Just like you cannot have a friend take your test for you, cannot have your friend qualify with a handgun for you, you also cannot have another officer write your reports for you.

One last introductory concept I want to address: I called this book *Professional Report Writing for Law Enforcement Officers* because I am not addressing only police reports. I am also referring to evidence logs, witness statements, confessions (if you write them for the subject), anything in narrative form, whether it be for jailers, investigators, probation officers; the topics I will discuss in this book will, frankly, be of value no matter your career. In fact, even if you end up working in another field completely, much of what you will learn in this book will apply with equal importance.

Chapter 1: Getting Your Voice

Think back to college, or perhaps high school, when you learned about voice. We are going to focus on the two main voices used in our kind of writing: active and passive.

Compare the following:

I was told by the witness that a loud crash was heard, then a crowd of people were seen running past him.
The witness said he heard a loud crash, then a crowd of people went running past him.

Does the longer sentence give you more information? Does it somehow make the information more clear, or easier to digest? Does it sound more formal? Does it just sound better? I don't think so! In fact, the passive voice makes it a murkier, hazier story. Read the two examples again. *A crowd of people were seen running....* By whom? The witness? Someone else? In fact, is it clear that it was the witness who observed these events? Technically speaking, the witness could be saying that someone told him these facts. To put it simply: passive voice lacks precision and you should avoid it.

Now compare another set:

A witness statement was collected by me, then the report was written.
I collected the witness statement, then wrote the report.

In the first example, do you know with any degree of certainty who wrote the report? Is it clear whether it was the writer of the sentence? That report could have been written by anyone. Just like the first set of examples, does the lengthier statement somehow give us more information? No! In fact, the longer sentence adds nothing but ambiguity.

This is a good (albeit loose) example of a concept generally referred to as Occam's Razor. Occam's Razor stands for the principle that generally speaking, the simplest solution is usually the correct one. I see the issue of voice as one conducive to analysis with something close to Occam's Razor: I recommend that we apply what I have dubbed Occam's cousin Wilhelm's Razor: the simplest language is usually the best way to describe something. (Do not expect an academic to have ever heard of Wilhelm's Razor; I just made it up!)

Applying Wilhelm's Razor in the two examples I provided, the shorter and simpler sentences are the more clear, easier to comprehend ones. You cannot go wrong using the active voice. They are almost always shorter and more clear.

Just as Occam's Razor can generally be applied in almost every issue you encounter, our new friend Wilhelm's Razor will also be relevant in just about all writing. Let's restate Wilhelm's Razor one more time: the simplest language is usually the best way to describe something.

One more quick comment on Wilhelm's Razor: some of you may be intellectual giants; you may already have advanced degrees. Many of you may actually be smarter and better educated than your supervisor, or at least the person responsible for reviewing and approving your reports. With that as a backdrop, consider the following two examples:

The witness elucidated that the suspect appeared to be hoary headed and devoid of facial hair. The suspect brandished a dirk of golden hue, and demanded that I divest myself of my wallet.
The witness said the suspect had gray hair and was clean shaven. The suspect had a gold knife and demanded my wallet.

I promise you that there will be many readers of your report that will require a dictionary to figure out the first example. It serves no purpose to use a more complicated word when a more simple one if available. Describing a suspect as devoid of facial hair gives the reader no more information than describing him as being clean shaven. Unless there is a legitimate need, do not use complicated words.

Sometimes you must use complicated words:

I searched the car and found drugs under the seat.
I searched the car and found methamphetamine under the seat.

I think you get the picture.

In professional report writing, the goal is to make your writing simple, to the point, and devoid of mistakes, exaggeration or personal opinion (or at least limit the personal opinion). Some of the most famous writers in the world wrote entire literary works with nary a three syllable word. Think of Ernest Hemingway. His lean, direct writing style made him famous. When you are writing, think lean and direct. Use short words and short sentences.

So avoid passive voice. What else am I talking about when it comes to voice? A good report does not require many adjectives or adverbs, very few superlatives, and no slang (more on this topic in the chapter devoted to Cop Speak). Let's take a look at Wilhelm's Razor in action:

Driver 1 proceeded through the intersection and was involved in a traffic collision with Driver 2, who was also proceeding through the intersection. Both Driver 1 and Driver 2 stated that they perceived a green light indicating their right to proceed through the intersection. Driver 1 and Driver 2 collided in the intersection, both claiming they had the green light.

So tell me this: which statement gives you more information? The first one? Read them carefully, and you will see they both give you the same details. The difference is that the second statement gives you the same information in 16 words that the first statement took 44 words to describe.

Let's review one more selection, this time an excerpt from a DUI arrest.

The drunk stumbled out of his car and blabbered something that sounded really stupid, then fell over on the ground. He was cuffed and stuffed by me.
The driver stumbled out his car, muttered something unintelligible, then fell over on the ground. I handcuffed him and secured him in the back of my patrol car.

The first example violates just about all the rules. The writer documented his personal opinion ("the drunk," "sounded really stupid"), used slang ("cuffed and stuffed"), and the passive voice ("cuffed and stuffed by me"). The personal opinion here serves no real purpose but to editorialize and suggest that you, as a witness, may even have a personal bias against drunk drivers. Nobody likes drunk drivers, but calling him a drunk and calling his behavior stupid does not further the criminal case and will guarantee an extra twenty minutes for you under cross examination.

QUICK TIP:

Many departments still handwrite the majority of their reports. Some departments have on-board computer systems into which you can type your reports. Some states still require specific forms for traffic collisions that must be printed in hand writing. Either way, professional writing will be important. A unique problem in using a computer is relying too much on spell check, grammar check and similar tools. In many cases, these programs are just plain wrong. If you don't understand the rules that these programs apply, then you will not know when to ignore the computer and when to correct the mistakes it finds. This is especially true when dealing with words that are spelled differently based on context:

The book is over there.
It is their book.
They're coming to get the book.
Spell check will probably not be able to distinguish between these spellings.

This book is designed to do more than prepare you to write police reports; it is designed to prepare you to properly complete any and all professional writing. You should be able to apply what you are learning here to even an evidence slip that requires nothing more than a signature. With that said, no matter what you are writing, and no matter the medium or the purpose, you should avoid having your handwriting look like the prescription your doctor hands you. You know the prescriptions I am talking about; the ones that always leave you with a look of amazement when the pharmacist glances at it and actually understands it. When completing a form, writing a narrative, even merely signing a document, there should be no question as to its content. Clarity is King.

In sum, use active voice whenever possible, avoid jargon, slang and avoid documenting your personal opinions unless they are conclusory and have value. For example: *I determined that the driver was less safe.* Or perhaps: *I placed him under arrest because I believed he remained a threat to his family.* To write *I arrested the stupid drunk* would be an improper documentation of your personal opinion.

Another concern in professional report writing is tense. You should avoid using present tense in your report writing. It is grammatically incorrect and awkward:

The witness says that he saw the suspect smashing the window.
I order the suspect out of the car

As a general rule, you should write in the past tense:

The witness said that he saw the suspect smash the window.
I ordered the suspect out of the car.

When relaying the facts to you, witnesses will often speak in present tense. When describing traumatic events, sometimes a witness will drift into present tense as they relive those traumatic events. To the extent you are recording verbatim quotes, the use of present tense may be appropriate. Witnesses giving you a statement in present tense is unavoidable. However, when you are the speaker, or the actor about whom you are writing, the use of past tense is more correct:

I ordered the suspect out of the car.
After checking the intersection, I drove down Mulberry Street.

By the time you are writing your report, the action you are describing, the statements you are recording, have already occurred. Past tense should be the tense of choice in all professional report writing.

In close, your report writing should generally be in active voice and past tense.

Chapter 2: Attribution

Let's briefly revisit our example from Chapter 1 and our friends Frank and Jones.

Frank told me that he told him Jones killed her, but not her friend. Frank said he last saw Jones at the corner of Fifth and Pine walking away from him holding a gun. Frank said that as he walked past that intersection he encountered Louise, and heard her tell him that Megan called him a jerk. Frank heard him tell her that he would kill her and that she was a bitch.

Frank said that Jones told Frank that Jones killed Jane, but not Megan. Frank said that he last saw Jones at the corner of Fifth and Pine walking south holding a gun. Frank said that as Jones walked past that intersection he encountered Louise, and Frank heard Louise tell Jones that Megan called him a jerk. Frank heard Jones tell Louise that he would kill Megan and that Megan was a bitch.

One of the main problems here is that of attribution. Attribution is the proper identification of the speaker of a statement, the doer of a deed, even a quality of a thing. In professional report writing for law enforcement officers, pronouns are the antithesis of attribution. *She, He, Him, Her, They, Their*, are all pronouns that can make a professional report confusing or even downright unintelligible.

How many times has someone said to you: "you know, they say that if you suck on a penny it will mess up the reading on a breath test" or "hey, they say that locking your doors improves the structural integrity of your car by 20%." I had a law school professor who would call on students by surprise during class. An unprepared student sometimes answered by saying "they say…." We have all begun a sentence with "they say…." Well, this professor would not accept such an answer. His response was usually something like this:

"They? They? Who is they? Why do I care what 'they' have to say?"

In short: pronouns are bad. References to pronouns might work for social conversations, but not professional report writing.

Let us now dig a little deeper.

There is another issue here, one that straddles both the topics of attribution and voice: it comes most often in affidavits. When writing about one's own action, LEOs tend to refer to themselves in third person:

Officer Starklight then detained him.
Your Affiant then detained him.

If I am writing this report, then it would be more clear, and easier to read, to say:

I then detained the driver.

Or, even better:

I detained the driver.

The interesting thing to note here is that the better sentence is both more specific and more general. If I am writing the report, and my name is at the bottom of that report, then there is really no reason to refer to myself by name.

Officer Starklight then detained him.

On the other hand, to whom does *him* refer? In context, it would likely be the driver. However, why leave such things to chance? If you are the speaker, refer to yourself as *I*. However, the object of your action in the sentence, *him*, should be more specific: *the driver*.

Also of note: the word *then* does nothing for the sentence. We like to fill blank space with words. Humans cannot stand silence. The next time you are interviewing a suspect, ask him or her a question and just wait. Don't say a word. The majority of people will not be able to handle the silence and try to fill it. Once you are aware of this concept, you will be amazed how often your fellow LEOs also cannot help themselves. Adding *"I guess"* to an answer, or *"Well, . . ."* or ending a sentence with *"you know what I mean?"* These are all gap fillers that have no useful purpose.

The same thing obtains on the written page: when writing professionally and with precision, you should scrutinize every single word and if it is neither required nor useful, you should get rid of it.

I then decided that, well, I might as well arrest him and place him in custody.
I decided to arrest him.

Does the first sentence give the reader anything more than the second? In fact, is even the second sentence as precise as it could be?

I arrested him.

Isn't that even cleaner?

Attribution is relevant for affidavits, for incident reports, and is most important when documenting witness statements, confessions and the like. When documenting the statements of others, always make sure it is perfectly clear to the reader who said what.

One theme that you can apply in your writing (and when providing testimony) is to imagine the way you would speak in social, semi-formal settings. I say semi-formal because when you are at a picnic with your friends, your language would likely be filled with slang and improper grammar, not to mention a lot of "you know what I mean" and "they say…." However, if you are at the office Christmas party and speaking with the police chief, you would most likely try to speak with proper grammar, avoid slang, and maintain subject-verb agreement. That is how your reports should read and how your testimony should sound.

This is a fairly straightforward topic, so let's look at a few examples of proper and improper attribution. These examples should be illustrative of the problems that can accrue:

I pulled him over and he yelled "it wasn't me!"
I pulled the driver over and the passenger yelled "it wasn't me!"

I chased him into the tree-line after he yelled "screw you, pig!"
I chased the male into the tree-line after his wife yelled "screw you, pig!"

A unique problem with attribution is that by failing to provide it in everything you write, you risk yourself forgetting who made the statements you recorded. I have written affidavits that do not become relevant in a case until years later. In re-reading my own words, I sometimes have difficulty recalling the speaker of some of the statements I recorded. If not for the prosecutor, then do it for yourself! You will write (and probably already are writing) reports every day. Day after day, month after month, into years, sometimes cases take a very long time to proceed through the judicial system. Do you think that once the criminal case is over that you are done? Guess again!

WAR STORY

I worked a traffic collision, citing both drivers because, in my estimation, both were at fault. At trial, the judge decided to dismiss both citations and let the insurance companies fight it out. I figured that was the end of it. In fact, years later, after I left the department to go to law school, I received a telephone call from a civil lawyer. Naturally, the insurance companies were unable to settle the claims, and the case ended up in litigation. Several years later, long after the criminal case was dismissed, this civil case was preparing for trial. I was subpoenaed to provide deposition testimony. I had no real recollection about anything, and barely remembered taking the accident report that was provided to me during the deposition. In short; my deposition was probably not very helpful to anyone. It brings to mind the classic (and comical) joke about the standard DUI reports submitted by old school state patrol officers throughout the nation: "*Saw drunk. Arrested same.*"

In my example here, it would have been a good idea for me to have taken a more complete report, quoting witnesses, quoting the drivers, describing with better detail the scene upon my arrival, but instead, I took a fairly bland, non-descriptive report. The case suffered for it, and I was somewhat embarrassed years later sitting in my videotaped deposition. During those days when I was a police officer, we were short handed, and I recall being dispatched from one collision to another, going from call to call with no break. We did not have the time to take detailed reports, and that is an issue with which many departments and many officers must cope. Ideally, at the end of the shift, an officer will spend the extra time to make all his or her reports as accurate and detailed as possible so they will remember what happened months, or possibly even years later. As a practical matter, that is not always possible. For that reason, my suggestion is this: take as much time as you possibly can to produce a detailed, correct report. Go the extra mile in making sure it is accurate and complete. It will pay you dividends in the long run.

Chapter 3: Cop Speak

Every LEO has spoken in cop speak at some point in their career. After the end of shift, at the local bar, how many of you have shared a story about a 10-80, or about a "44 in progress?" You cannot help it! This is cop speak. Good radio discipline requires the use of signals and codes, but when documenting your actions in a report, you should avoid cop speak. That means refraining from the use of signals, codes, and police lingo. Some of that lingo is obvious and should be avoided: *perp, code 4, low sick.*

Sometimes cop speak is not only acceptable, but necessary to properly describe your behavior:

I Mirandized the suspect.
I read the driver the Implied Consent Warning.

The key is to know the difference between necessary lingo/cop speak and unnecessary. One good rule of thumb: if someone who is not a LEO can read your report and understand it, then it might be ok. Think of one of your parents reading your report. Mom and Dad will probably understand that you Mirandized someone, but will probably not know the difference between a Signal 2 and a Signal 3 (where I come from, it is the difference between an audible and silent alarm).

Certain phrases like the two I used above (*Miranda, Implied Consent)* are necessary. They are not slang or a contraction (*perp = perpetrator*). They are technical terms, or words of art. There is no other way to refer to them without greatly lengthening your report, and they have become a part of common understanding in the community. By the way, that concept of being woven into the fabric of society is so important that the United States Supreme Court cited it as one of the reasons why Miranda could not be overruled!

So in short, certain examples of cop speak are so ingrained that their usage has become popular enough to make them acceptable, and as we learned with Wilhelm's Razor, these phrases are much more concise than having to describe the concept. Imagine the following:

I read the suspect his rights as guaranteed to him under the Fourth Amendment of the United States Constitution and memorialized in the United States Supreme Court case of Miranda v. Arizona. *I informed him of his right to remain silent, his right to have counsel appointed....*

Isn't it easier to just say:

I Mirandized the suspect.

I think you get the idea.

Another trap LEOs fall into is stilted, stuffy, formal language. This is a particularly insidious subset of cop speak, because they are all normal, non-law-enforcement type words that have been adopted by the law enforcement community. Let's look at an example:

I proceeded through the parking lot, where dispatch had advised the complainant was waiting.

This might be a touchy section. Some of you have probably incorporated much of the contents of this chapter into your daily report writing, and will be clutching these old favorites to your chest as I ask you to give them up. Take a deep breath, then say your last "advised" or "proceeded" and let them go. In the immortal (and sometimes disputed) words of William Faulkner, you must "kill your darlings." In other words, those words to which people clutch so dearly are almost always the ones that need to be eliminated. Faulkner was referring to characters in books of fiction, but the premise is the same.

Back to our example:

I proceeded through the parking lot, where dispatch had advised the complainant was waiting.

This sentence has two main problems. It is written in passive voice, which is fertile ground for cop speak. Let's take this one apart.

Number one on the chopping block is *advised*. You are a LEO, not a lawyer. You aren't really in the advising business. When you tell someone something, you are doing exactly that. Your job is to make decisions and give direction. Rarely is it your job to provide advice. Generally speaking, perhaps 90% of the time, when you write in a report that you advised someone of something, you really just *told* them something. Don't glamorize it by calling it advice.

Furthermore, it is the very rare occasion when someone on a dispatch advises you of anything. The victim did not advise you of his injuries; he *told* you about his injuries. People tell each other many things, and on your dispatches or law enforcement activities, few will be truly *advising* you.

Proceeded is number two on my naughty list. The driver didn't proceed through the intersection; he drove through it. The jaywalker didn't proceed across the street; he walked! It is not incorrect in usage, but it is stilted and too general. People walk, people drive, people fly. People rarely proceed, at least not in ordinary usage. When was the last time you told someone that you proceeded somewhere? If someone walked, write that they walked; if they ran, write that they ran; if they drove through the intersection, then that is what you should write!

Also, eliminate the use of proceeded as a preparatory verb:

I proceeded to drive through the intersection.

This reminds me of my friends in the south, who are always "fixing" to do something.

I'm fixing to go out to eat.
I am proceeding to go out to eat.

Do these preparatory verbs really do anything to either sentence? Arguably, one could say *"I'm about to go out to eat."* That at least informs the reader that you intend to go out to eat shortly. *"I am preparing to go out to eat"* is better. *"I am proceeding to go out to eat"* sounds like you are doing it right now. It is imprecise and unnecessary.

Remember Wilhelm's Razor? Wilhelm's Razor would call for the elimination of "proceeding" in just about every sentence. It adds nothing but fluff and an air of stuffy formality. When someone asks you for directions, have you ever told them to proceed to the next street and turn left? Well, some of you probably have!

Stuffy: He fled on foot.
Better: He ran away.

Stuffy: They had an altercation.
Better: They had a verbal argument/physical fight.

Stuffy: He sustained a cut to his face.
Better: He was cut on his face.

Stuffy: I transported him to the hospital.
Better: I drove him to the hospital.

Stuffy: The victim was Code 4 at the scene.
Better: The victim was unharmed at the scene.

I think you get the picture, but before we move on, let me just mention one more word that you should eliminate from much of your professional writing: *Observed*. Mis-using this word makes a sentence too stuffy and vague.

I observed the victim had a cut to her face.
I observed the vehicle parked in the handicap parking spot.

Try these instead:

The victim had a cut to her face.
The vehicle was parked in the handicap parking lot.

Here are a few more:

I observed the vehicle drive by.

Try instead: *I saw/watched the vehicle drive by.*

I observed that he was shuffling his feet.

Try instead: *He was shuffling his feet.*

As you can see, Wilhelm's Razor would call for the elimination of *observed* in virtually all of these examples. *Observed* is only appropriate if it is important to describe that you personally witnessed something as it occurred:

I observed the driver back into the fire hydrant.

The word *observed* is similar to *proceeded* in that it is almost always mere filler; it does nothing but make a sentence bulkier. These words are the written equivalent of those little white Styrofoam peanuts that come in packaging materials. Leave them in the box and only pull out the valuables they were protecting! Only use them when they are absolutely necessary.

There is another subset of vocabulary commonly used by LEOs that need to be excised from professional report writing: words that aren't really words at all. The greatest offenders for LEOs are "*supposably*" and "*irregardless*." Perhaps I am old fashioned, but I refuse to accept these as real words. The legitimacy of the word "*Irregardless*" has been disputed for almost 100 years, and if a word has not made it into accepted usage in a century, there is no good reason to accept it now. As for *supposably*, it is, arguably, a word, but it has no place in the usages most commonly applied to it in professional writing. Do yourself, and the readers of your written word, a big favor, and get rid of these words. And while you are at it, toss "*exspecially*" in the can with them!

Slang and what I would call police vernacular also have no place in professional report writing. *Perp, bad guy, coms, vic.* These, and any iterations of them, should be avoided. *Perpetrator, suspect, subject, communications, victim*, these are neutral and acceptable. Perp is an improper shortening of perpetrator, and bad guy imparts a personal opinion that has no place in your report. You are not a made-for-television character like Officer Sipowitz from *Law and Order.* You are a professional LEO. Do not call suspects perps. Do you refer to other officers as *cops* in your reports? I have never seen it used. (By the way, do you know how police officers acquired the nickname *cop*? It is actually an abbreviation for *constable on patrol*.)

"*I could care less.*" Ok, this is not an issue for professional writing, but it is a big one in speaking. If you can care less, that means in the grand scheme of not caring, there are many things that you dislike even more. 99% of the time, the speaker means to say "I could not care less," meaning that the thing to which the speaker refers is the very bottom on his list of things to care about.

Another confusion in terminology that I often hear, and one violated by a few lawyers I know: *moot* and *mute.* These two words have virtually nothing in common. It is almost never *a mute point.* A person that cannot speak is never *moot.* Let me give you just one example of correct usage for these two words.

It is a moot point because she already fled the scene.
The witness, a deaf mute, provided a written statement.

I have just a few more that I have heard in my time that I will address here. We are straying somewhat from the point of this chapter, but it will benefit you to read this section, and hopefully you will get a little laugh out of it.

Kick him to the curve. A famous comment made by motor officers nationwide. It generally means to perform a traffic stop. Unfortunately, it makes no sense. I can only assume the correct phrase is "kick him to the curb." If you must use such a phrase, at least say it correctly.

He was lit like a roman candle. Or, *he was a drunk.*

This could be a chapter in itself. When documenting someone's intoxication, use descriptive words, not conclusions or slang. In the incident report documenting a DUI arrest, your evidence that a driver was intoxicated is his slurred speech, his nystagmus at maximum deviation, his failure to successfully complete whichever field sobriety tests you administered. You should not document that he is *drunk, lit, toasted, shit faced, hammered* or anything similar. Just find and record the facts, your observations, and don't editorialize. Let the prosecutor make conclusions and charging decisions based on your evidence. Here is a thought: if the word you want to use to describe an intoxicated suspect is one that you have used when referring to yourself while out at a bar, it is probably not appropriate.

By the way, please indulge me with a slight diversion here. When an incident you investigated goes to trial, you will give the prosecutor a copy of your report. The prosecutor, through discovery, will hand a copy over to the defense. You will be questioned about your report and cross-examined about your report. So many of you might ask, what is the role of the incident report in a trial? Generally speaking, it is not evidence. It is not admissible as evidence in a criminal trial because it is hearsay. However, it *can* be used as the source of cross examination. It *can* be used by you as a testifying witness to refresh your recollection. It *will not* be admitted into evidence. The Rules of Evidence are beyond the scope of this book, and those rules are somewhat different in every state, so citing the rule of one state will not help those of you in any other state. For our discussion, just know that your report is not evidence but can (and will) be used against you!

QUICK TIP

I briefly touched on this earlier, but let me reiterate this point. Don't use cop speak in court. Jurors are more likely to connect with you, the arresting or citing officer, than they are with the lawyers. One of the main reasons jurors want to be on your side is that the jury considers the prosecutors and defense attorneys as part of the whole judicial system, along with the judge, the bailiff, and the other various personnel staffing a courtroom. Most of what comes out of the lawyers' and judge's mouths are unintelligible to the jury, a confusing and somewhat theatrical play acted out in a courtroom. They are the furniture in the courtroom. Their focus is on you.

The whole point of jury instructions prior to deliberation is to "dumb down" and explain the law the jury must apply when reaching their verdict. It is somewhat insulting as a juror to find that they are not trusted to simply read and apply the relevant statutes. You, as the star witness for the government, should not provide testimony that requires the jury to refer to a dictionary. To connect with them, your testimony must be simple, detailed and straightforward. After all, rare is the juror who "proceeds" to court to sit in the jury box. They *want* to like you and connect with you. Make it easy for them!

One more little diversion into the realm of courtroom testimony. Remember that law professor I mentioned earlier? He had another pet peeve with his students: the use of "I guess."

When a student started his response to a question of his and started with "I guess," it normally solicited a response from this professor close to the following:

"You guess? You guess? Are you paying all that money to go to law school to sit here and guess? If I want people to sit in my classroom and guess, I will just go pull a few of those landscapers outside into my class, sit them down right here in the front row and let them guess all day long. Are you a lawyer or a landscaper?"

And that student would never say "I guess" ever again.

Here is a free rule about courtroom testimony: never say you guess. Your guess is not admissible as evidence anyway, and it will anger many law school professors! Guessing is tantamount to speculation, and speculation is inadmissible in court.

Chapter 4: Distractions

This chapter is, in a sense, an expansion of everything else about which I have already written. All the issues we have discussed can each create distractions for your readers. Something we have not yet addressed that can be very distracting are simple mistakes. Typographical errors, misspellings, improper spacing, these can all distract the reader from the thrust of your writing. As a uniform patrolman, my reports had to be turned in before the end of my shift. Detectives have more time to complete their reports: they can document their investigation, set it aside, and review it the next day, with a fresh eye. Once you complete a report, ideally, you should set it aside and review it one more time for accuracy after letting some time pass. If you do not have this luxury, then you will have to review it for errors as soon as you finish writing it. You must teach yourself this discipline.

Back when I was writing incident reports, I wrote them in long hand and had to press down because we used three copy reports. If I misspelled a word or made a mistake my choices were to scribble out and try again, use liquid paper, or crumble it up and start over. If I chose liquid paper, I had to use three bottles, each a different color. White for the original, blue for the detective copy, pink for the third copy, the purpose for which I cannot remember.

In any event, it was understandable when an officer just scribbled out a word. These days, given the use of computers, mistakes are less tolerable.

As a general rule, your written work product should be perfect in every way. You should make that your goal. Limit the time you spend wishing you had added some fact, or left out something irrelevant. Limit the time spent listening to a defense attorney cross examining you about some imprecise statement you had placed in your incident report.

Avoid abbreviations. Your sergeant might understand them and approve your report for filing, but not the prosecutor, the defense attorney, the court, or the jurors.

I transported him to ADC.
I obtained a 10-17 for the suspect.
The arrestee kicked my MDT.

Try instead:

I drove him to the adult detention center (or jail).
I obtained a warrant for the suspect.
The arrestee kicked my mobile data terminal (or computer).

QUICK TIP

Here is another good reason to proofread your work: did you know that your reports may be subject to your state's open records act or sunshine act? The federal government has the Freedom of Information Act, which allows anyone to get a copy of a public record merely by asking for it. Just because a case you made has been resolved does not mean that your reports will not remain available for many years thereafter. A good defense attorney, in an effort to defend his client and make you look like a sloppy LEO, may file an open records request and review copies of every other arrest report you have ever made. If you are a sloppy writer, that could become a real problem. Do not place yourself in the position of having to defend your writing in court.

Here is another good reason: if you were to be sued for something you did as a LEO, the plaintiff's lawyer will demand, subpoena or request everything you have ever written. If your written work product contains careless errors, that lawyer will portray you as a sloppy officer that cuts corners and does not pay attention. Is that the reputation you want to have spread about regarding your work ethic? Minimize the criticism someone can lodge against you. Proofread your writing. Even Shakespeare has something relevant to contribute here:

"The evil that men do lives after them, The good is oft interred with their bones." (Julius Caesar, Act 3, Scene 2.)

A few days after you do something on the job, the only evidence left of your actions will be your written word. You could do all the right things on a dispatch, but if you do not properly record those things with your report writing, the only thing people will remember, or be exposed to in reviewing your work ,is your documentation of your good deeds.

So, exactly which facts do you put in the report? Everything that is relevant. It is like the famous question asked of a famous sculptor: How do you take a block of marble and turn it into a gladiator on a chariot? The sculptor's answer: It is simple; I take my chisel and remove all the rock that does not belong and what is left is the gladiator on the chariot.

Leave out irrelevant details. Tell the whole story. Try to avoid making personal conclusions or giving personal opinions. One caveat regarding irrelevant details: I tend to document as much as I can because I want to be able to recall the incident. A year or two down the road when a certain case finally goes to trial, I will have to refresh my recollection of that incident, what people said, what I did, what exactly happened. Better to take an accurate, lengthy report and preserve your ability to recall the facts, than to have a bare bones report that gives the basics but not enough detail to give you the power of recall.

Take copious notes. Try to keep them. If your department has a method (or requirement) for storing them, use it. As a police officer I had a duffle bag filled with my old note pads . I had one in my back pocket my entire time on patrol, and everything I did went into those pads. Even after the passage of twenty years, I can open up one of those pads and instantly recall much of the dispatches during which I took those notes.

Those notes will make the difference from a barely acceptable incident report and one that tells the whole story and gives you the recollection you need to testify. The more you write, the better off you (and your reports) will be.

Use contractions sparingly, if at all. They generally have no place in professional report writing. Don't, can't, won't, shouldn't, these are not incorrect and not slang, but are informal and therefore inappropriate. You will find an occasional contraction in this book. However, this book is not an official report. It was designed to be informal to make it more readable. In professional report writing, however, contractions should be avoided. Imagine contractions in other professional documents.

This contract is legally binding; the parties can't derogate from the terms.
If the defendant doesn't report to probation, a warrant will be issued.

Do those quotes sound like they came from a binding contract or court order? How about these:

This contract is legally binding; the parties shall not derogate from the terms.
If the defendant does not (or fails to) report to probation, a warrant will be issued.

At the other end of the spectrum from contractions are long quotes. Avoid them. If you put something in quotation marks, you are indicating that what you wrote is exactly what the speaker said. Perhaps if you have a recording of the speaker, you will be in a better position to accurately quote the material. If the speaker says something particularly important, by all means quote it. The issue here is whether you should ever quote entire statements.

Let me make a suggestion: if you have the speaker on tape, then why not quote only the most important, most relevant parts, and forget the rest? If the person's entire statement is that important, then have someone else (or do it yourself) just transcribe the entire interview.

Here is another alternative: just burn the recording onto a CD and maintain it somewhere until the case is over. Again, you must refer to your agency's policies as to what you can do. My main point here is that if you must quote someone, make sure it is accurate. It is difficult to accurately quote someone, and that is why I suggest you avoid it. An example will better illustrate this point.

When I was a patrolman, upon the arrest of a driver suspected of DUI, we were required by state law to read what was called the Implied Consent Warning. We all carried little cards around, and read straight from them, our little belt mounted recorders busily recording our words and the driver's answer. Those cards seemed to change every few months, in direct response to court cases in which the language was successfully challenged. The cards changed color, and the dates were printed prominently upon them. Some officers wrote out the exact language of the card from which they were reading. I never did this, as it seemed unnecessary, and even worse, one single error in that language and you would find yourself in a long and painful cross examination trying to explain whether you read exactly from the card or whether you said exactly what you wrote in your incident report. Many of us kept all the old cards in a safe place in case a DUI arrest went to trial. I thought it was much better an idea to refer to the color and date of the card from which you read, and keep a copy of that card in case you did go to trial.

What is my point in the above paragraph? Do not directly quote something or someone unless you are not only certain of the quote, but confident that the quote itself is crucial to the successful resolution of your case.

Chapter 5: Improving Your Writing

Over time, practicing your professional writing will itself improve your professional writing. This may be somewhat of a syllogism, but it bears noting here. Writing improves over time. However, what do you think is the number one way to improve your ability to write? Reading!

Try to read every day. Read whatever you want. Read for pleasure. You won't even realize your writing skills are improving with every word you read. Your vocabulary will improve. You will recognize awkward writing, misspellings, improper tense, subject verb agreement; these mistakes will be as obvious as if they were printed in a different color.

Be an active reader. The meaning of many unfamiliar words will be clear from the context in which they are used. Those that do not reveal their true meaning should be looked up in a dictionary. If you are using an e-reader, you may even be able to just click the word and link straight to its definition. Technology is slowly removing any excuses you may have for not *actively* reading more often.

Also, write as much as you can. E-mails probably count if you try to make them real prose and not glorified text messages. Keep a journal. Write a short story or a letter to an editor. Your writing will improve. Get a pen pal. If you intend to start (or finish) college, try to take courses that require a lot of reading and writing. Such work will pay off dividends. If you are currently a college student, enroll in the courses that require term papers or at least regular writing assignments. The feedback you receive will be well worth it. If your agency offers training in report writing, take it. I would tell you to send me some of your reports for a critique, but I would quickly be overwhelmed by the response and my mailbox isn't big enough!

Go to a bookstore (or online) and buy *The Elements of Style* by William Strunk, Jr. and E. B. White (most popularly: "Strunk and White"). It is a short, pithy list of linguistic right and wrong and a requirement for any educated person's bookshelf. It is no bigger than *Grammar Saves Lives* and almost as easy to read. Let me give you one theme from this absolute-must-have book: *Eliminate needless words.* Needless words unnecessarily lengthens your writing and distracts the reader.

There are a few great websites that discuss redundant language, and there is a lot of it in professional law enforcement writing. Here are a few, straight out of the Department of Redundancy Department:

ATM machine= automated teller machine machine.
Completely eliminated = is there only a little bit eliminated?
The victim was completely dead = can one be partially dead?

Check out http://grammar.about.com/od/words/a/redundancies.htm. The title of this web page is *200 Common Redundancies.* The author, Richard Nordquist, lists these examples and many others.

The Internet is your friend. Many has been the time that, having forgotten a specific rule, I have typed a question into a search window on the Internet and 90% of the time, the first hit is the answer to my question. For example: what is the difference between e.g. and i.e.? Let's consider this a test. Type the preceding sentence into Google and click on the first result. I bet it gives you the answer. (If you do not have the Internet, just wait until the next page.)

There are a few other common errors you must avoid and that are always confusing. Luckily, these errors are so common that all you need to do is type the words into Google and press enter. The ones I see the most are *their* and *there, we're* and *were,* and *it's* and *its,* and so on. Do not be afraid to look up these words. These days, most LEOs have a smartphone and can get the answers to these questions while sitting in a patrol car. In my day, we carried dictionaries in our pursuit cases. These days, all you need is an I-Phone!

Those are some good general ideas. Now let's talk about some specifics to keep in mind when writing your report.

Common Errors

I considered not including these issues in the hopes of streamlining this book. However, these errors are so common, so distracting, that I decided to include them here. Let's start with my earlier example ,
e.g. and i.e.

Exempli gratia (e.g.) is Latin for "for example."
Id est (i.e.) is Latin for "that is."

My favorite cars are old American muscle cars, e.g., Mustangs, Chevelles, Cougars.
This is my favorite car; i.e., the Mustang.

There and Their

There tells you where. *Their* is possessive.

The suspects are over there.
These are their burglary tools.

Since and Because

Since involves time. Because tells you why.

He said he had been drunk since last Thursday.
Because you asked me, I will tell you.

It's and Its

It's is a contraction.

Its shows possession.

It's going to be a long night.
The dog chased its tail.

Could of Would of Could have Would have

Could of/Would of are just plain wrong.

I could have seen him if I had my glasses.
She would have gone to the gym if she was feeling better.

Organization / Consistency

Pick an order. It doesn't matter how you choose to organize your report, as long as it is organized in some fashion and that you are consistent with it. A lot of this section is dependent on your agency's paperwork, reporting requirements and general practice. I will try to stick with concepts that will be applicable to any situation.

In a prior career, long before law enforcement, I received some training as a forms consultant. There is actually quite a bit of thought that goes into the creation of a form for a business. In my experience, there are many law enforcement agencies that seem to put no thought at all into their layout. For example, have you ever noticed forms that contain a blank space for one's age that is twice the size as the blank space for one's name or address?

My point is this: do not assume that your agency's forms will cover all the relevant information that should be in the report itself. If there are boxes to fill to document a suspect's height, weight, hair color, eye color, build, complexion, race, gender, that is all useful information. However, if you just stick with the form information, you are doing your case a disservice. Was the suspect angry? Did he speak a foreign language? Did he have (or sustain) visible injuries during the crime? These are data that may be crucial to solving your case, but if you do not go the extra mile and document these observations, your case will suffer.

Perhaps the best example for this concept is the standard DUI report. Many agencies have tried to cover all the bases with their forms. There is a box to check for almost every observation, including every field sobriety test (FST) you could think of, and the results. These are great cues for an officer trying to cover everything. However, nothing beats a good, descriptive narrative. Checking boxes does not tell the whole story. People cannot "read" little check marks. People want to read a story, not hunt for little check marks. And, by the way, just checking boxes leaves a lot of information off the page. For example: which FST did you request from the driver first? Then which one? What if something strange happens during one of the FSTs? Is there a place to document observations on each one? That may need to go in your narrative.

So let's return to organization. Chronological order makes sense. What happened first? Then what happened? Then what? That sounds simple enough, right? Well, the question is upon which chronology will you rely? Let's say you have been promoted to detective (congratulations!) and have just completed a multiple witness, multiple day investigation. You now have an idea of what happened. For our example, say someone's home was burglarized, and you interviewed ten people in ten days. Let's also say that the victim has had someone living with them for two months and suspects they were involved. How do you order your report?

One method of chronological organization is to start with your first interview, then your next, then your next. In other words, your chronological organization is based on the interviews you conducted. This makes sense because it documents your interviews in the order you conducted them, which makes it clear why you didn't know to ask certain questions of your earlier victims, and why your knowledge of the facts improves the further into your investigation you go. Someone else can read your reporting and watch your investigation unfold.

On the other hand, reporting your investigation chronologically in this fashion can really muddle things up; your first witness could be the one that saw something suspicious the day after the burglary and the next witness could be someone that knew the roommate twenty years earlier. A reader new to the material might get lost very quickly.

You could also take all your witness statements, then write the report chronologically as to what happened. So here, your first paragraph might discuss the roommate moving in and why, then move on toward the suspicious activity of that roommate in the days before the burglary, then the burglary, then the aftermath. This paints a clear picture and lets an unprepared reader jump right in. The criticism for this approach is that it is much more difficult to organize because you must sort through all your witness statements and break them down into the right spot in your report. This can cause problems because it is much more prone to mistakes and can easily become very choppy to read.

Avoid duplication. I have seen investigations at certain agencies in which the investigator continually adds to his original report, and incorporates the narratives of his interview reports into this original report. This can get very confusing, especially for readers not familiar with the investigation. Further, the investigator never has a complete report. It will always be a work in progress.

There are other possibilities, although frankly, one of the above is generally your best bet. There are also some hybrids that take from both types of chronological interviews, then borrow from some other angles. Some LEOs may provide an introductory paragraph that lays out the complaint and the conclusion, then all the supporting facts. Other LEOs stick to the program, putting all the interviews into his or her report and moving on. As I mentioned earlier, the important thing is that you are consistent, and that other people can read your material and know exactly what happened.

There is one more comment on organization that I would like to share with you. Consider documenting your interviews and your investigative activity separately. One interview goes on one report; one investigative act goes in another. For example, you interviewed ten witnesses, so that is ten interview reports. You may have dusted the victim's home for prints, so that is one report. Then, say, you generated some leads and showed the witnesses some six packs. That would go on another interview report. Once you are finished with your investigation, you could gather up all your reports, then sit down and draft a narrative that combines all the salient features of your investigation. As you can imagine, this document could become your prosecutive memorandum, your probable cause statement for your arrest warrant, or your affidavit for a search warrant. In this manner you can minimize your duplicative work and focus on documenting what you are doing one time, then consolidate all that work at the end of the case.

No matter how you choose (or are told) to organize your writing, your reports will benefit greatly from taking proper notes during interviews and during investigations. The more complete and detailed your notes are, the better your report will be. In the case of a long investigation, those notes will be crucial in reconstituting all the information you have gleaned.

Do not rehash your entire investigation with each subsequent report. Many LEOs believe they must constantly add to their investigation as if they were adding chapters to a single novel. The first report they write may be a page, and the second two pages, and by the end of the investigation their reports are over 100 pages each. Perhaps this is personal opinion, but I fail to see the benefit to this method. The argument in favor of this method is that each report can stand on its own, and that if all the other reports are lost or destroyed, the reader will know the entire story from the most recent report.

There are several criticisms for this method. Here are two: first, with each new iteration of your report, you will have a larger number of former versions. Those versions may have found their way into many hands; supervisors, judges, attorneys. How will one know if they are looking at the most recent version? Second, the longer someone has to read to catch up to the new material, the less inclined they will be to read it. If you have a report that is twenty pages long and add two sentences to document subsequent information, you now must print a twenty one page report. Seems like a waste, doesn't it?

My perspective is as follows: if someone is reading one of my reports, the probability is very high that they already know why they are reading the report and the underlying facts that led to me writing it. Imagine how much unnecessary writing (and subsequent reading) would be required if, when documenting witness interview number ten in your burglary case, you had to summarize the entire investigation. It is simply not necessary. Anyone that wants to catch up with your case can read the previous reporting in your case file.

What if a week after you complete your investigation, you uncover new evidence, or a new witness appears with new information? Most agencies have some kind of addendum form or additional narrative form. Use one. Do not try to add the information to a report you already turned in. As long as the report file number is marked on the page, you should not need to rehash your entire investigation. This is especially relevant if you had a very long investigation, and/or the additional information is either of minimal use or minimal length.

Structure

Another thing that can be not only distracting but make it difficult to read your written word is that of structure. Long, run on sentences can kill someone's interest in reading your material. If you have not yet noticed, the paragraphs I have written in this book are intentionally very short. It makes for an easier, more pleasant reading experience, and should be incorporated into all professional law enforcement writing. If a paragraph is more than four or five sentences, there is a problem. That paragraph must be simplified and shrunk. I am not saying to eliminate the actual material; merely to shorten your paragraphs.

As a general rule, a paragraph should only contain one idea or one situation. For every new idea or situation, there should be a new paragraph. In professional report writing, it is best to minimize the length of your paragraphs. If you have a single idea or situation to document and you are exceeding three of four sentences, scrutinize your paragraph closely; chances are, you can break it down into smaller chunks. The point is to make it more digestible for the reader.

If you have a lot of paragraphs, consider adding sub-headings. You will have a hard time engaging a reader faced with a sea of words with no guideposts. If you have a very long investigative report, such as in the case of a murder investigation, the final product may require a table of contents. Do not make a prosecutor have to thumb through dozens of pages looking for what they need. How do you think you would enjoy this book if I failed to use sub-headings and chapters?

Details

The details of your reports will be very important. So what should be included in those details? I will try not to address police procedure, but one of the biggest examples of the importance in attending to details is in the suspect description. Think of the sculptor chiseling the gladiator on the chariot: put in everything that belongs and nothing that doesn't.

When you are drafting an incident report in which you have a witness providing a description of the suspect, that description should be very precise. That means asking the right questions so you can get the information you need. Perhaps the witness only saw the suspect for a second or two. Perhaps it was dark and they only saw a shadow. Do not simply become a recording device, writing down what you are told and moving on. You must dig. Witnesses are just that; witnesses are lay persons generally not accustomed to paying the level of attention to their environment like a LEO does. You will need to pry, poke, prod and ask round-about questions to get to the heart of the memories.

Say, for example, your witness is an elderly person and she is trying to explain the time of day she witnessed a suspect crawling into her neighbor's window. The elderly person states only that it was daytime. How can you pinpoint a better time estimate? What questions could you ask? Try asking your witness what they were doing at the time. Ask what was on the television, or whether she was taking any medication that day ,whether she was eating and if so, what was she eating? The answers to these questions are completely irrelevant to the crime you are investigating. However, they are clues to when the crime occurred, and these odd questions will trigger memories that she may not find relevant, but will be excellent guide posts for you to arrive at a proper time estimate. If *Murder, She Wrote* was at the point where the heroine discovers the killer, then you know it was in the last five minutes of the hour in which that show was televised (unless your witness used Tivo, in which case you will need to try something else).

My commentary here is dangerously close to police procedure, and I don't want to tell you how to do your job; only how to write about it. The reason I brought up the questions to ask witnesses is to emphasize that some of these seemingly innocuous questions and their answers may become very important later. Read the following excerpt from a report:

The witness said she saw the suspect knocking on her neighbor's door, wait for a few minutes, then disappear. At that time, the witness was watching the beginning of Murder, She Wrote. *Later, as the show was ending, she saw the suspect walking around from her neighbor's back yard and climb into the back seat of a blue truck. The witness said she does not own a VCR or any other device that records television shows. The witness has Charter Cable.*

Ninety percent of the excerpt above has nothing to do with actual suspect information. However, it provides the prosecutor with some valuable information that will support and enhance the testimony of this witness when and if the case goes to trial. It provides enough information for one to establish fairly accurately when the suspect arrived and left, and almost exactly how long he was there. It also explains why the witness was able to recall the time that she saw the suspect. Should this information be in your report? Of course!

Something else that is important to keep in mind when documenting your interactions with witnesses: witnesses have five senses, and they all can provide useful information and all of their relevant sensory observations should be recorded. Observations can be equally and sometimes even more important than language.

Language can be subject to hearsay exceptions or a privilege, but observations are non-testimonial and almost always admissible as long as they are relevant. *Always document observations*. In the example of a DUI arrest, describe the driver's *appearance*: disheveled, red eyes, slurred speech, stumbling. Describe his *odor:* he reeked of alcoholic beverage. If your agency permits you to record witness statements, even better. Keep in mind, however, that they may very well be inadmissible unless you can get that witness to testify. If the witness is unavailable and you are called on to provide testimony regarding your interview of a witness, these additional details will help you immensely. If you are a busy LEO, you will not be able to testify adequately without recording these little details.

Given the importance of observations, and the rules of evidence regarding hearsay, know that your descriptions of what you see and hear are very important. Witness statements are good, but if you get those statements, make sure you get accurate contact and identifying information for those witnesses. If you cannot find them later to testify in trial, their statements may very well be out of reach.

Statements made by a defendant is one important exception to hearsay. You might hear such statements referred to as statements made against one's penal interest, confessions or admissions. If you have such evidence, make sure you properly document it.

Forms

Much of your professional writing will be written into or upon forms. Arrest reports, accident reports, evidence forms, contact cards, they will all have boxes requesting certain information. As a general matter, the purpose for such blocks is to guarantee that your report contains the most obvious data needed for the case. These blocks may require the name of the complainant, the address of the incident, a description of the suspect, etc. Some agencies have fairly detailed sections that require completion. Some are quite complex, and even confusing (see the section on **Organization**).

If you are providing certain information in these sections of the form, you should strongly consider omitting that information from your narrative. For example, if the suspect portion of the form already contains his height, weight, gender, hair and eye color, clothing, mannerisms, and demeanor, then those descriptors probably do not require further attention in your narrative. These sections all make up a single form. You should save the narrative portion for additional information not already contained elsewhere in your report. Use the narrative to tell the story and add unique information that was not already captured elsewhere. You could describe the suspect as follows:

The suspect, <u>as described above</u>, appeared very agitated and had a bleeding injury above his left eye.

Some officers simply do not complete the fill-in-the-blank portion of their reports, preferring to document everything in the narrative. That may be ok in some agencies, but understand that many agencies use the fill-in-the-blank portions for data collection, mandatory reporting, and analysis. This data collection can be very useful: analysts can review burglaries agency/county/state/nation wide and match suspects based on common data. If you leave these fields blank, your data will not be captured and your case may go unsolved because the report did not provide that data for analysis.

Beyond Reporting

Not all LEOs are first responders writing incident reports in their patrol cars. Many of you may need to draft affidavits, declarations and other documents, some of which will be eventually signed by a judge. This is an especially important subset of professional writing that you must master. Some of you will have the benefit of a prosecutor reviewing this writing and making the necessary corrections. Whether or not you have this benefit, your writing should be precise and free from errors.

You should apply all the rules we have discussed in this book. Avoid stilted and overly formal language. The one to watch out for in this context is referring to yourself as *Your Affiant*. Just say *I*. The judge knows you are the Affiant! It will significantly reduce space and make for a much more readable document.

Always describe your relevant experience and education in the beginning of your affidavit. This is a chance for you to introduce yourself to the court and to explain why the judge should believe you. Some jurisdictions have particular rules. Some jurisdictions require the affiant to be a state certified peace officer. If so, you must lay out that you meet the requirements to submit affidavits. Some LEOs call this their "hero sheet," and lay out all their particular training and experience. Whatever you call it, make it complete, complimentary, and relevant, and above all else, make sure you provide everything the judge will need to approve whatever you are asking for, whether it be an arrest warrant, search warrant or the like.

Remember, you will swear to the fact that everything contained therein is a true and accurate statement. Make sure you can honestly swear to that fact. This is not the time to be sloppy in your professional writing. There could be serious consequences for not taking sufficient time drafting this document. If you have someone helping you draft or edit your work, make doubly sure that you have read the final version very carefully before signing it and swearing to its veracity. Your reputation, and thus your career, depends on this.

A Word About E-writing

E-mails, text messages, PIN messages, SMS, even voice mails, anything digital that records something you are saying or writing, requires particular attention. These are communications that can stick around on someone's hard drive for years, unbeknownst to anyone. You must be careful with these mediums for communication. The most common mistake is speaking too casually, and without regard to the fact that these communications can actually be discoverable. E-mail exchanges between LEOs regarding cases are actually statements and will most likely have to be given to the defense when and if the case is charged and goes to trial.

Should you avoid abbreviations and lingo in these communications? Of course not; you only have so many characters you can type into a text message. These are not formal communications. You simply need to get a certain point across when sending a text. However, you should use caution with these mediums, as they are prone to be taken lightly; abbreviate as needed, just do not cross the line.

Furthermore, if an e-mail you send gets forwarded to someone else, eventually it could end up in the hands of someone you do not expect; from there it could find its way into a newspaper or defense attorney's inbox. For these reasons, you must make sure that you treat these communications as carefully as you do your affidavits, reports, and all the other mediums we discussed. Do not write in these mediums in a manner that suggests prejudice, uses foul or inappropriate language, or in any way could be used to discredit you or harm your reputation for speaking the truth.

These documents are generally not maintained as carefully as official documents, and could therefore be altered. Furthermore, they can survive far longer than some official records that are subject to destruction rules. In short: treat every communication as if they were going to be later read by a defense attorney, or your supervisor, or your spouse. If you would not tell these people in person what you are writing, then do not write it! I know more than one LEO that simply does not send text messages or e-mails. When you send one of these electronic messages to them, you get a telephone call in response. Think of it this way; if you are responsible for the arrest of a very wealthy person, that person will be willing to pay some private investigator a lot of money to dig up dirt on you. Do not let them have anything to find.

Final Thoughts

Once you have completed your professional writing, put it down. Walk away. Take some time if you have it. Return to it only after you have cleared your head. Then you should read it again, looking for mistakes, clarity, accuracy. Editing and proofreading is just as important as writing the report. The final product should be perfect.

I had an Evidence professor in law school who used to tell us that every year he sat in his office and read the Federal Rules of Evidence from cover to cover. He knew the rules by heart, but explained to us that every year he discovered some nuance, some language that he had not noticed before. It is like the preacher reading the Bible every day. Years and years later, that preacher may still find passages that suddenly seem relevant, or have some meaning not considered previously. This is one of the reasons why it is so important to read, re-read, then re-read again. This applies to your own reporting. If you write a report, review it immediately, then hand it in for processing, you are cheating yourself out of the ability to look at the document with fresh eyes. You will gloss over your own mistakes.

Additional Resources

There is a great website I have found called Wisc-Online. The website was created by faculty at the Wisconsin Technical College Program and it has some great ideas and resources. They actually have an interactive police report writing program that you can use. Try it at http://www.wisc-online.com. When you get there, click on the button marked "learning objects." Then look on the left for a drop down menu titled "General Education." Then click "Technical Reporting." You will then see the program, "Investigation Report Writing."

Here is another really fun website, sponsored by the publishing company Wadsworth. It is a template for a police report. The web link is very long, so do this: do a Google search for "Wadsworth" and "police report template." It will be your first hit. This website has an actual Microsoft Word version of a generic police report. There is no feedback on this one, but if you are new to law enforcement, you will find the exercise of completing a report worthwhile.

Even the website WikiHow has something to say about police report writing: http://www.wikihow.com/Write-a-Police-Report. Of course, Google is also in the mix and has collected dozens of police reports and related forms and templates here: http://website-tools.net/google-keyword/word/sample+police+report+template. This one is especially interesting, as it features forms and samples from all over the United States and overseas. Do a little research on your own and you will find an unlimited amount of resources on this topic.

I hope you have enjoyed this little book and learned something from it. If you are considering a career in law enforcement but have not yet embarked on your journey, pick up a copy of *How to Become a Police Officer: The Best Tactics to Get Police Officer Jobs and enter the Police Academy*, and you can get some good, straight forward advice on how to start that journey.

If you just want a little entertainment and maybe get some insight into the daily life of a uniformed beat cop, you will soon be able to check out my other book, *Police Daily Journal; Tongue in Cheek True Stories.* These are true stories about true events. I personally experienced each of them, and tried to select those that are indicative of what some of your first dispatches may be like. I also tried to use only those that provided some entertainment or comedic value. Like I have said before, you must find the humor in being a LEO. If you take yourself too seriously all the time, this job will weigh you down and cause emotional damage. Go to the end of my book and click the button to add your e-mail to my mailing list. I'll let you know when the book is released.

I wish you all the best of luck and am confident that if you paid attention to the content of this book, your writing will improve starting right now!

\# \# \#

If you enjoyed reading this book, I hope you consider taking a look at some of my other books: *How to Become a Police Officer: The Best Tactics to Get Police Officer Jobs and enter the Police Academy.* And, coming in August 2020, *Grammar Saves Lives, Volume 2!*

Following is an excerpt from my book in progress, *Police Daily Journal; Tongue in Cheek True Stories:*

Excerpt from *Police Daily Journal; Tongue in Cheek True Stories*:

Day 8

Today I was assigned to our 344 beat, which meant I would spend almost my entire shift going from one silly call to another. 344 was a somewhat narrow but very long beat: I could spend the evening driving from one end of it to the other. What made it worse was that it was almost all strip malls and expensive neighborhoods with no highways. There would be nothing except for false residential alarms, accidents and silly disputes.

Furthermore, the officer assigned to 344 beat was partnered with the one assigned to 346 beat, and I knew that 346 would be empty for a while. The officer assigned to that beat had a reputation for sticking around the precinct for at least an hour after everyone else was in service. There was always a reason; "I had to discuss something with the Sergeant," or "I had to finish some paperwork before I left," or "I had to return a few calls from yesterday." Whatever the case, he was always the last officer in service. If you were his beat partner, you knew you would be handling things for yourself all evening.

As I will learn today, sometimes it doesn't always help to treat people with respect. Today, as I walked into the squad room, fifteen minutes early, my Sergeant was waiting for me. A dispute in progress was just announced over the radio in my beat, and the beat cop on the day shift was in court and could not respond. There was no-one to go except me and my friend Victor, who was in 348 that day; we had both arrived early to the precinct. We each grabbed a set of keys off the board and ran out the door. We were in service within five minutes and asked the dispatcher for the details. Apparently a pair of landlords were trying to kick out their tenants for failure to pay their rent on time. Alcohol was involved and the tenants were scared.

This was a problematic call for the police for several reasons. First and foremost, police officers cannot enforce contracts, or become involved in civil matters. If a tenant signs a lease with a landlord and then fails to pay the rent, the remedy is whatever is contemplated in the lease. Generally, the failure to pay rent leads to an eviction, which is a civil remedy. Police officers cannot enforce such a remedy. When dispatched to such a call, it usually infuriated the landlord to learn that we would be unable to assist them. This becomes even more problematic when alcohol is involved and when the dispute becomes immediate and physical. The dispatcher said we had all of the above.

It took us a while to find the house. It was all the way in the back of a very nice, very ritzy neighborhood. There were a lot of cul-de-sac streets and loops and traffic circles. Not an easy house to find. Once we did, we saw a Lexus in the driveway parked askew and the front door to the home was wide open. My partner and I cautiously approached and found a woman in the foyer in her fifties along with a much older woman, at least eighty years old, standing with a cane. At the top of a flight of stairs was a young foreign couple (turned out they were French) standing together, clearly frightened.

As we walked in we could clearly smell the unmistakable odor of an alcoholic beverage. It seemed to be coming from the women in the foyer. As we entered the room, the woman in her fifties turned to us and became quite animated. She was taller than me and quite portly.

"Good! The police are here. Go arrest them!"

With that, the woman grabbed me by the arm as if to launch me up the stairs. As a uniform police officer, it is quite offensive to be grabbed by someone. As she made her exclamation, it was clear that her breath was the source of the alcohol smell.

I tried to calm her down, but it was nearly impossible. I determined from her comments that she and her mother were at a bar when they decided to call their tenants and order them to be gone before they arrived back home. When they finally did leave the bar and found the tenants still there, the landlord/homeowners went ballistic. There had been no formal lease signed; the agreement was all oral. The tenants, who were in the United States on student visas, had not paid the rent because their sponsoring university abroad had been late depositing their stipend in their bank accounts.

I tried to explain that we could not enforce a lease or an eviction, and this succeeded only in making the woman more upset, louder, and more physical. She again grabbed my arm as if to send me vaulting upstairs. I pulled my arm away and warned her that the next time she touched me she was going to be arrested for battery. She didn't listen to me.

During this exchange, my partner, Victor, was standing by the woman's mother. The mother, it turned out, was also drunk, and was teetering on her little collapsible walking cane. She was silent, just watching the events unfold.

The younger woman made one more move toward my arm and grabbed it. I had had enough, and I yelled at her that she was under arrest. Apparently she did not want to be arrested. I had to wrestle her to the ground. Meanwhile, my partner was watching me with his mouth open, surprised perhaps that I was going to arrest her, or that she was resisting arrest, or maybe a little of both.

While he was watching in disbelief, the woman's 80-ish year old mother slid into action. She shuffled by my partner and up to the melee going on at her feet. I noticed her movement out of the corner of my eye, and turned to her just in time to see her with her arms over her head, clutching her collapsible cane, which she slammed down right between my eyes. That hurt! The cane collapsed, and as she reared up to hit me again, I did the only thing I could think of: I grabbed the younger woman in a one-armed bear hug, then grabbed the older woman by the shoulder. I pushed her backward toward my partner as hard as I could. She didn't weigh too much, and slammed into him and came to a landing at the foot of the stairs. I then finished wrestling the younger woman into handcuffs.

But it was far from over. We called for an ambulance for the older woman, but the younger one was still in the fight. She was trying to kick me, bite me, spit at me, whatever it took to get her revenge. Eventually I had to roll her onto her stomach and literally sit on her back. I was able, finally, to get the hand cuffs on her, but I had to remain sitting on her back like a bull rider. We waited for the ambulance to respond.

I thought that time would allow her head to clear somewhat, but I was wrong. The fire department arrived with the ambulance, and an old fire Lieutenant swaggered into the home. He had a long, old fashioned handlebar moustache, and had the general appearance of a cowboy from the Wild West. The Lieutenant asked to take a look at the woman I was sitting on, so without standing up, I crouched down and told her that the fire department was here and wanted to make sure she was not injured. I asked her if she was going to allow them to check on her welfare, and she nodded her assent. She was still panting and grunting, though. The Lieutenant approached, I stood up from her and helped her sit on the floor, and without pause, she somehow managed to lie back on her side and as hard as she could, kicked the Lieutenant in his private parts. He fell to the ground beside me, and I had to sit back down on the defendant. In the end, it took four of us to get her into the ambulance. At the jail, she was so brutal that she was strapped into something they called "The Chair." It was a chair that strapped the seated party at the head, chest, arms, legs and feet. She tried biting every deputy that came within two feet. I am honestly not sure what happened to the older woman; I only remember her complaining to the EMTs that I might have broken her hip.

After leaving them at the jail, I had to drive to the Magistrate's Office. I will explain this in more detail on another day, but generally speaking, when a police officer charged someone with a crime (with certain exceptions, like traffic code violations), that officer had a short window of time within which they had to go before a judge and prove that there was probable cause to support the arrest. That judge (in Georgia) was called a Magistrate. I intended to charge them both with battery, which, under Georgia law, meant any offensive touching. It was a misdemeanor, and included kicking someone, grabbing them, or biting them. Georgia also had a crime entitled aggravated assault that, in Georgia, essentially meant threatening to use or actually using a deadly weapon against another. This was a felony. In both cases, there were special provisions if they were committed upon a police officer or fireman.

I wasn't a big advocate of charging an old woman with aggravated assault on a peace officer (a police officer in Georgia is called, by statute, a peace officer), but when I explained what happened to the Magistrate, she informed me that the facts fit the offense and it was the most appropriate crime with which to charge her. That evening, I left her office with two felony warrants with multiple charges for their attack on me and the Fire Lieutenant. It was a little embarrassing, but only a little. What was even more embarrassing was the Polaroid my Sergeant took of my face when I returned to the precinct that night. I had a large goose egg right between my eyes and on my forehead from where I was struck with the cane. It was entered as evidence for my case.

I learned a lot from that encounter. I think the most obvious lesson was that even little old ladies can hurt you. If her walking cane was one inch to the left or right, I might have lost an eye. An officer can never, ever, let their guard down. With the right amount of alcohol and a little anger, even someone's grandmother could be pushed over the edge and might attack you.

I also learned that an officer may do themselves a disservice to try to downplay the criminal behavior of another. I had nothing to be embarrassed about by charging an 82 year old woman with a crime. What happened today was clearly a felony, and not a misdemeanor. I was physically attacked by someone with a weapon. That was a textbook case of aggravated assault. It was the responsibility of the Magistrate to determine whether there existed probable cause to support my allegation that a crime was committed, and it was clear from the facts that there was an aggravated assault. It would be up to the district attorney's office to determine the proper charges and punishment for that offense, and if that meant offering to let the old lady plea to a reduced offense and a light sentence, then so be it. We each had a role to play in the criminal justice system; mine was to report the facts and the prosecutor's was to prosecute. In this case, that is exactly what they did.

Other Books to Read

by Steven Starklight

How to Become a Police Officer: The Best Tactics to Get Police Officer Jobs and enter the Police Academy

Grammar Saves Lives, Volume 2 (Available in August 2020)

Golem

By Jonathan B. Zeitlin

Death and Repair; a Michael Hart Mystery

The Body in the Hole; The Undertaker Series, Book 1

The Body in the Bed; The Undertaker Series, Book 2

STEVEN STARKLIGHT
GRAMMAR
SAVES
LIVES
PROFESSIONAL WRITING FOR
LAW ENFORCEMENT OFFICERS
VOLUME
2

Grammar Saves Lives!

Professional Writing for Law Enforcement Officers

Volume 2

By Steven Starklight

Introduction

The first volume of Grammar Saves Lives was published in 2012 and it was a much bigger hit than I expected. I wanted to write a brief guide that was short and sweet, serious but entertaining. I saw a lot of textbook-style guides on the market, long and boring, with lots of exercises. I knew that's not what you all were looking for.

It's been a long time since I sat in a patrol car. Back then, if a law enforcement officer (henceforth, LEO), needed a book on writing, they had to go to the bookstore and find it on the shelves. They would have to remember to stick it in their pursuit case, and if they were walking a foot beat, they would have to carry the book around with them.

Well, now it's 2020. Everyone has smartphones. You need a book about writing? You can find one and download it from your patrol car. Or from the booking room. Or while standing on a street corner.

I figure many of you will want to read this book in your patrol car, or in the jail, or while watching television. That's why there's no fancy pictures, no diagrams, no exercises, just the basics, written in a format anyone can read. Who cares about dangling participles, gerunds, and diagramming sentences? You need the basics.

When I worked in Washington, DC, those of us commuting to work on a Metro train used e-readers or phones to read books during the trip, and we wanted something easy that you could pick up and put down without losing the story. A "light read." That's why I intended here. You can read a couple pages between calls, put it down for a while, and pick up where you left off. Each chapter and sub-part can stand on its own. Easy.

Volume Two builds on Volume One. In other words, I tried very hard not to repeat myself. I didn't just rewrite the first book to make more money. (Let's be honest, book sales are not going to be a meaningful part of my retirement income.) Volume One covered a lot of material, but after eight years, I realize there are quite a few additional topics worth covering.

My two books on writing, combined, are not even close to being a "complete" guide to every grammar rule. If that's what you are looking for, I encourage you to browse around the Internet and you will find many options. They are much bigger books than mine, and they are a lot more expensive. They will teach you everything you ever needed to know. They will have diagrams, photos, test questions, reading assignments; it will be like going back to school and sitting through English class. Lots of them are hard cover, also making them effective blunt edged weapons in case you need to defend yourself.

Look at it this way: say I'm the rangemaster at your department's range and I'm writing a short book about shooting technique. Let's say the book is called *Guns Save Lives*. For that book, I am assuming each of you already own a firearm, and that someone has already taught you the basics. You already generally understand gun safety, how to clean your weapon, nomenclature, and you can usually pass the qualifications course- but you could do better. If you reliably shoot 80%, perhaps my book would get you to 90%. Maybe you'd even hit 95%.

Anyway, I thought long and hard about what rules are most commonly violated, and which of those violated rules cause LEOs the most problems. I tried to limit my lessons only to those rules. That means my volumes are a fraction of the size (and price!) of most of their competition, yet I think they cover the majority of the most common mistakes.

Seriously, both volumes will total less than the cost of any of those other textbooks out there. But if that's not good enough, I'll make a deal with you: if you buy this book and like it, leave me an honest review on Amazon. Once it posts, email me at stevenstarklight@yahoo.com and tell me which one is yours, and I will send you the first volume for free. Deal?

The subtitle to both volumes of Grammar Saves Lives is "Professional Writing for Law Enforcement Officers." I am not here only to write about grammar. In this volume, I am going to touch on issues that go beyond grammar and delve into professional writing in general. One can write a technically perfect document that is, nevertheless, terrible. Writing is like shooting- even if you follow all the rules, you can still shoot a terrible target.

For this volume, I am trying a slightly different format, with less stories, and more guidance. My goal is to give you some ideas that will apply to incident reports, but also will help you with writing sworn statements, whether in support of an arrest warrant, search warrant, wiretap, or just about anything else that a judge will read. I also added a special bonus section for supervisors.

I focus on grammar issues at a microscopic level, then zoom out to share a few broad ideas I want you to think about as you are writing. I want to keep things interesting, so I will spread these broad ideas throughout the book so things don't get too dull. Let me start with a broad idea.

Part One

1.   Telling the Story

I named this chapter Telling the Story, but in fact, you never want anything you write in this line of work to be a story. It has to be the truth and only the truth. Each sentence should contain a fact, and that fact should be verifiable in some way. When I write an affidavit, whether for a search warrant or some other kind of sworn statement, I always make sure I can prove each fact. When I am writing the first or second draft, I usually add footnotes for each sentence, and each footnote is a reference to a source document or thing: an interview report, a piece of evidence, a statement of a witness. You get the picture.

The judge never sees that footnoted version; I remove them from the final copy. Federal agents have been doing something similar for many years. When federal agents submit an application for electronic surveillance under the Foreign Intelligence Surveillance Act, or "FISA," they follow something called the "Woods Procedures." In each FISA application, the federal agent has to create a "Woods File," and in that file, the agent must document the source of every fact alleged in the FISA application.

Procedures like maintaining a Woods file ensures a LEO's application relies only on facts that can be sourced and supported with evidence. Unless you are applying for a FISA, you need not worry about keeping a Woods file, but keep it in the back of your mind when you are writing your reports and your sworn statements. Make sure you know the origin of every fact in your investigations, and be prepared to cite them. Unless you have a photographic memory, you should consider how you will remember the source of all those facts years later when you may have to give testimony about those facts.

Facts are important. Without them, all you have are opinions. Facts in your head are memories, and memories are perishable. You don't have to keep a Woods file, however. I will cover this within the section **Affidavits**, and give you some good ideas how you can never worry about forgetting those details when it comes time to testify in court. Now, on to our first concept:

A. State the Facts

This rule, **State the Facts**, is one of the most important. As a LEO, you should be reporting facts. There are also certain situations where you can give opinions.

I named this section Telling the Story, but to be accurate, the only people in a criminal case that should be telling a story are lawyers. They tell a jury what they expect the evidence will show during opening statement, then they tell the jury what they think happened when the trial is over during closing argument. Those are stories, nothing more. Neither opening statements nor closing arguments are evidence.

Only the jury can decide which story (the prosecution or the defense) was closer to the actual truth. But remember: nothing coming out of those lawyers' mouths are evidence, and the jury cannot use any of it in determining the guilt or innocence of a suspect.

Witnesses don't get to tell stories. LEOs are witnesses. You can tell stories outside of work. Tell stories to your family. Tell stories to your friends over drinks. Tell stories to a suspect you're interviewing. But you should never tell anything but the truth when you are in court and under oath. Tell only the facts. Well, that's not entirely true. Sometimes, under certain circumstances, you can also share opinions.

Yes, I said it, sometimes LEOs can share their opinions. You can write them in incident reports, affidavits, and accident reports. Think about a DUI. Applying my first rule, Tell the Facts, you will write things like the following:

"I asked Driver to take ten steps forward, heel to toe.
After three steps he tripped and fell flat on his face."

"I asked Driver to submit to a breathalyzer test, but Driver
refused."

"Driver's eyes were red and bloodshot, and there was an
empty beer can on the seat beside him."

As anyone who has executed a traffic stop on a possible drunk driver knows, you reach a point in your investigation when you make up your mind either to arrest them or not. If you do, that means you believe you have probable cause to believe the driver is drunk. That's where your opinion is important.

"Having observed the driver fail successfully to complete
any of the sobriety tests, and based on my training and
experience, I determined the driver was under the
influence of alcohol and placed him under arrest."

There is nothing wrong with a LEO providing his or her expert opinion in this case. In fact, it's the LEO's job to determine whether the driver is less safe, and that *requires* the rendering of an opinion.

How about one more example:

"When I arrived at the home, the woman was holding ice
to a large bruise on her left cheek. The man was
attempting to leave the home. He had blood on the
knuckles of his right hand, and his breath smelled like
metabolized alcoholic beverage."

What do you think?

"Based on the bruising on the victim's face and the
injuries to the suspect's knuckles and his attempt to flee
the scene, I determined he was the primary aggressor and
I arrested him for simple battery."

How does a LEO decide whether there is probable cause to arrest someone? It requires the LEO to form an opinion.

Opinions are perfectly acceptable, as long as they are supported by facts. Facts will include your observations and your experience. Your observations will include what other people tell you. I will cover all of this in a little more detail later in the chapter, "**Affidavits**."

B. Use Exact Quotes

Let's talk about taking statements from others. As I just wrote in the last paragraph, your observations include things other people tell you. When you record what other people tell you, you must be as accurate as possible.

This isn't a book about how to interview witnesses, but let me say this about taking someone's statement: be accurate, be complete, and if you can collect some good quotes, you should record them *exactly as they are said*. Be certain when you take the statement. Repeat the words to the speaker if you wish. Consider documenting the fact you read the statement back to them. Do what it takes to make sure the statement was accurately recorded.

I have interviewed suspects for whom English was a second language, and in some cases, I had them write out their own statement and sign it. I have typed statements into my laptop and read them back to the witness. I have tape recorded them. You should do whatever it takes to ensure the accuracy of the record you create.

> **PRO TIP**: Establish a habit for yourself. *Always* document exact quotes made by witnesses, victims, and especially suspects. Place them within quotation marks. Avoid using quotation marks for anything else. One day you might forget the moment when the witness made the statement, but you will be able to testify that you *always* recorded exact quotes by placing them within quotation marks, and you *never* paraphrase such statements. Forming such habits will make you a better witness in court.

Accuracy is crucial when you document statements of witnesses, suspects, and victims. A related issue is what I like to call *intentional inaccuracy*. You know the exact quote, but you don't want to write it, and/or you don't want to have to repeat it out loud.

This is no place for the squeamish. F-bombs, F-words, four letter words, words describing someone's mother: if the witness said it, you should write it, and you should record it accurately. Exact quotes should always be used. If you have them, use them, and put them within quotation marks. There are still officers that refuse to curse or use foul language. That's great, but if you are one of those officers, you must learn to reconcile your work with your beliefs. Let me explain.

If you are investigating a traffic collision, which of the below sentences is better:

"I measured really long skids before the point of impact."

"I measured 36.8 feet of skids before the point of impact."

This one is fairly obvious. Vague and ambiguous facts are barely facts at all. What do we know? In the first example, we know there were some skid marks. In the second example, we might have enough evidence to estimate the speed of the vehicle before impact.

How about this:

"The subject said, 'You wanna die tonight, bitch?"
"The subject said, 'You don't want any of this."

The first quote sounds like a threat, while the second could be the clerk at the bakery warning you the bread is stale.

This last example is part of a true story- an-off duty officer and his wife were driving to the store, and while they were stopped at a red light, the occupant of the car two lanes over got out, brandished a firearm, and made the first statement. The off-duty officer reached for his own firearm to stop the threat, but before the shooting started, another car pulled into the middle lane, separating the cop and the suspect, then the light turned green, and the suspect jumped back in his car. The off-duty officer recorded the license plate.

The off-duty officer called 911 and a state trooper came to take an incident report. The off-duty officer provided the trooper the plate number and the exact quote, above, and explained that he vividly remembered what the suspect said. Thanks to some good old fashioned police work (conducted by an agency other than the state police), the suspect was arrested and found guilty of assault.

Many months later, while preparing for trial, the prosecutor provided the off-duty officer a copy of the original incident report. It was the first time the off-duty officer saw it. To his surprise, instead of using the exact quote he was provided, the trooper wrote the second version. Thanks to the trooper's sloppy work, the off-duty officer spent almost two hours under cross examination about his memory, about his accuracy, about whether he was lying; you know the drill.

If a witness gives you an exact quote, use it, and don't change anything. If you are worried that one day you may be asked to testify and may have to repeat the quote, and perhaps you are worried about offending the jury or the judge, warn the court before answering the question. If you truly have a problem using such language, make sure you discuss it with the prosecutor well in advance. Either way, however, know that an *intentionally inaccurate* report like the trooper's report in the example above will come back to bite you later. Trust me. I was the off-duty officer in this example. If the trooper accurately recorded my statement, he and I would have spent hours less on the stand.

Tell the Facts is an important rule. But Tell the Facts is a necessary, but not sufficient, requirement. You have to tell the facts *with clarity:* tell them in a way that makes them easy to read. Here's a few more rules:

C. The Paragraph Rule

This one is easy. A paragraph, generally, should only say one thing. Consider this paragraph:

The witness said she was driving east bound on Main Street when she saw a blue Dodge run the red light southbound on Main at Oak and slam into the Ford truck. The driver of the Ford truck said he was passing through the intersection after getting the green light, and was hit in the driver's door area by the Dodge. The driver of the Dodge said he was southbound on Main approaching Oak and looked down to change the station on his radio, and when he looked up he saw he had the green light, but then saw a Ford truck in the intersection but he could not stop in time and hit it. He said he had had two beers while watching the game, and was on his way home.

That's a lot of material. Witness statements, at-fault driver statement, cars, streets, alcohol. Consider this, instead:

The witness said she was driving east bound on Main Street when she saw a blue Dodge run the red light southbound on Main at Oak and slam into the Ford truck.

-insert space-

The driver of the Ford truck said he was passing through the intersection after getting the green light, and was hit in the driver's door area by the Dodge.

-insert space-

The driver of the Dodge said he was southbound on Main approaching Oak and looked down to change the station on his radio, and when he looked up he saw he had the green light, but then saw a Ford truck in the intersection but he could not stop in time and hit it.

-insert space-

The driver of the Dodge said he had had two beers while watching the game, and was on his way home.

Pretty simple change, but it makes the report a lot more readable, doesn't it?

It's important to break down each paragraph into no more than a couple of facts, or one main concept, then move on. Some departments make you use forms that don't give you a lot of room to write. That's unfortunate, but you should do your best to make your report readable.

Always check- in almost every case, there are "continuation pages" or "narrative supplements" you can use to tell the whole story without worrying about running out of space.

There are a few reasons why the Paragraph Rule is important. Not only does it make your report easier to read, but it makes it more likely each fact you cite is noticed. Have you ever submitted a report, then had to endure a supervisor or prosecutor asking you twenty questions about the case, when the answers to those questions were all in your report? Have you ever wanted to scream at the questioner, "Did you even read my report?"

Don't bury all the facts in a mound of words. A properly written and laid out narrative will go a long way to minimize these frustrating experiences.

Being careful with paragraphs also helps you organize your own thoughts in a more logical fashion. This will be particularly helpful if that case you wrote about ever makes it into a courtroom, and especially if you must testify. Compare this:

> *"Officer, referring to your report, in which direction was the Dodge headed?"*

To this:

> *"Officer, referring to paragraph 1 of your report, in which direction was the Dodge headed?"*

Which question is going to lead to a much more quick and confident answer?

D. Atmospherics

Prosecutor: *"Remember that time, three years ago, when you responded to that crash at Pine and Elm?"*

You: *"No, sorry."*

Prosecutor: *"You know, the one with the Camaro and the Dodge Ram?"*

You: *"Sorry, I still don't remember."*

Prosecutor: *"Officer, would it refresh your recollection if I show you your report?"*

[approaches witness and provides the witness an accident report. Officer reviews the report.]

Does that sound familiar? Ever read one of your own reports from a year or two ago and have no memory of the incident? Let's do an exercise. Close your eyes, and think about an incident to which you responded. Think of one from a long time ago, but one that is still vivid, still fresh in your memory.

What about that incident was so memorable? Was it the types of cars involved? Was it the location? Or was it something more subtle? Maybe it was something totally irrelevant to the case that made it stick out in your mind. I like to call that stuff atmospherics.

Atmospherics might be the weather, what someone was wearing, maybe they had an accent, whether there was a big group of people having lunch at a patio restaurant. Whatever sticks in your mind on the day of the incident is probably worth recording. Some of it might also be relevant for your investigation; if it's raining, that is a potential contributing factor in a car crash, but not so much for a domestic. In the latter case, the weather might only be atmospherics.

Of course, your supervisor might order you to strike some of this stuff from your report, claiming it's irrelevant. Maybe that supervisor is right. Maybe you need to record such things elsewhere. I will cover this under the heading Your Back Pocket.

Let's use the same car crash example, but this time we will add some facts, in italics, to the story. Try to figure out what are facts and what are merely atmospherics.

The witness said she was driving east bound on Main Street when she saw a blue Dodge run the red light southbound on Main at Oak and slam into the Ford truck. *It was raining hard at the time. The Dodge already had damage to the front bumper before it hit the Ford. It had a bumper sticker that said Go Dawgs.* The witness noticed the driver of the Ford was on a cell phone when he was hit.

The driver of the Ford truck said he was passing through the intersection after getting the green light, and was hit in the driver's door area by the Dodge. *He denied being on his phone during the time of the accident.*

The driver of the Dodge said he was southbound on Main approaching Oak and looked down to change the station on his radio *because he hated listening to commercials,* and when he looked up he saw he had the green light, but then saw a Ford truck in the intersection but he could not stop in time and hit it. He said he had had two *warm* beers while watching the game, and was on his way home. *He said the Braves slammed the Orioles after Phil Niekro pitched an almost perfect game* (yes, it's been a long time since I watched baseball).

I took some liberties with this example. Can you tell which are relevant facts and which are atmospherics? Sometimes it's hard to tell the difference. The sentence about the driver denying that he had been using his phone is hearsay (see *Grammar Saves Lives, Volume 1*) but likely admissible under one of the statutory hearsay exceptions. The comment about the baseball game is totally irrelevant to the car crash, but it provides atmospherics that might trigger your memory when it's time for you to testify (see Your Back Pocket). The temperature of his beer is irrelevant (but may be atmospherics), as are his preferences about what played on the radio.

Imagine you were dispatched to this crash. You are holding your notepad and listening to each witness and driver give their statement. You're actively listening for relevant information to go into your report and to help you assign fault. Just about all the non-italicized information I gave you should probably go into your report. What about the stuff in italics? You will decide what, if any, of that information will be recorded. My advice is that regardless of what you think about the information and whether you intend to add it to your report, you should add it to your notes. I'll go into more detail in the section **In Your Back Pocket.**

There's an old story about a grizzly old state trooper taking a drunk to jail. He wrote the driver a ticket for DUI, and handed it to the jailer along with his probable cause statement: "Saw drunk. Arrested same." That might have been enough fifty years ago, but not now. I had a good laugh when I first heard that joke, but then I experienced it.

When I was a prosecutor, I acquired a case against a drug dealer who had been arrested by a state trooper during a traffic stop. The driver was charged with trafficking in methamphetamine. In Georgia, trafficking was a felony with a potential sentence of thirty years. It was a big case, right? There were no incident reports at all. There was a traffic citation for trafficking, a lab test confirming the methamphetamine, his booking information, and a three sentence application for arrest warrant. There was nothing else. What do you think that trooper will remember two years later if the case goes to trial?

So, in short, be aware of the concept of atmospherics, consider what information might trigger your memory in the future, and try to record that information, because those observations will help you not only remember what happened, but help you describe it so that a judge or jury will better understand.

This is a tough concept precisely because it is so dependent on the circumstances. Does it matter if it was raining? *Depends*. Does it matter what someone was wearing? *Maybe*. Does it matter why someone was driving in a certain direction? *Possibly*. My advice is to record everything in your notepad, but be judicious with atmospherics in your official report because there is a fine line between atmospherics and the dreaded concept of-

E. Surplusage

This is important. It might also be the most difficult thing to master. In the immortal words of William Strunk, Jr., "omit needless words." Strunk wrote *The Elements of Style* in 1918, and E.B. White expanded Strunk's book in 1959. Strunk and White's book should be required reading for anyone that uses a pen and paper. Or typewriter. Or computer. I cannot over-stress the value of this book. You should buy a copy. You should buy a copy now.

Omit needless words. Having unnecessary language in an incident report is like having a car with five wheels, or two brake pedals. What's the point? All they do is get in the way and distract you. Same thing goes with your sentences, paragraphs, and reports.

I'm sorry to be the one to say it, but there is only one way to improve on this one: revision. Write your report, then review it. Sentence by sentence, you need to read with a critical eye and make sure (1) there are no unnecessary words, and (2) the sentence actually says what you meant for it to say. Here's an example:

> *The driver then decided to say to me that really, he*
> *thought that the traffic light was not red, it was green,*
> *and that if he was paying more attention, he would have*
> *been able to avoid hitting the car that was in front of him.*

Of course you need to tell the story, but you can tell this story with much more clarity. Let's clean it up a little:

*The driver ~~then decided to say~~ [said] to me that ~~really,~~ he
thought ~~that~~ the traffic light was ~~not red, it was~~ green,
and ~~that~~ if he was paying more attention, he would have
been able to avoid hitting the car that was in front of him.*

That's a little better, but I think we can improve it even more. Try this:

*The driver believed the traffic light was green. He believed
he would have avoided the collision if he had been paying
more attention.*

This is a difficult rule. It is not about just making the sentence shorter. In fact, in some cases the sentence might be longer after a proper revision. But we aren't finished.

Read the second version again. Is it clear? Are there any unnecessary words? Could I have written it more clearly? In making it clearer, did I also make it more ambiguous? "The driver believed the traffic light was green." How do I know this? Did the driver actually say it? How did he say it?

Let's try it again:

*The driver said he believed the traffic light was green, and
that if he had been paying more attention, he would have
avoided the collision.*

Is that better?

You are probably saying to yourself, *What a tedious waste of time*! Trust me: you can spend the time now or you can spend the time later. If you write a vague and confusing report, you will pay for it in court, and I guarantee a thorough and sifting cross examination is far more painful than proofreading a report.

As an aside, this rule is very similar to what an old boss of mine called the Sixty Minutes Test. When considering whether to engage in any given behavior, first imagine that behavior being featured on the show Sixty Minutes. If you aren't excited about that behavior being broadcast to the world, maybe you should consider doing something else. Being a LEO means someone will always be watching what you do, and reading what you write. The less you give them to criticize, the better off you will be.

By the way, do you want to be famous? Did you know there are companies that travel the country visiting law enforcement agencies and courthouses and perusing reports and judicial opinions? Some do it on behalf of the media, while others do it for television and movie studios; either way, they are looking for things to talk about. I know this because I was once contacted by a certain television show featuring a "judge" who decided on small claims matters. This person wanted me to "testify" on their show regarding this case I investigated. (I said no.) Sometimes unscrupulous lawyers do this. You probably have heard of the phrase "ambulance chasers."

Side Note to Surplusage

When we talk about the elimination of needless words, we are really talking about the need for *clarity*. I'd like to add a few quick points here on clarity. These are points I should have made more strongly in Volume 1.

F. Contractions

I touched on this subject in Volume 1, but it bears repetition and expansion.

Contractions very rarely have a place in professional writing. Other than quotations, you should avoid them. You might notice I have used them here and in Volume 1. This is a classic case of do what I say, not what I do. I really wanted this book not to be stuffy and clinical like so many other books on writing. A modest sprinkling of contractions helps lighten up the topic. However, when writing professionally, you should avoid them. Also, remember, I won't ever have to testify about the contents of this book!

G. The Royal Comma

Let's move on to something sexy. Yes, I said it. Punctuation can be sexy. We will start with the Royal Comma.

Actually, there is no such thing as a royal comma. There is the serial comma, also known as the Oxford comma, but that is but one of several comma rules that I have seen wantonly violated in books, magazines, web pages, and the like. I have titled this section the Royal Comma because it is one of the most frequently misused or missing punctuation marks in the English language, along with the humble apostrophe. (Please disregard my anthropomorphizing the apostrophe.)

Maybe you're a cop sitting in a patrol car scrolling through my book on your tablet or phone, and I am guessing you probably don't care about what the proper name of this comma is, or the actual rule, you just don't want to violate it. So here's the deal: a comma separates clauses in sentences, or items in a list.

If you don't tell me your real name, you are going to go to jail.

In the back seat of the car, I found a bag of marijuana, a pack of Marlboros, and a vial of pills.

The Oxford comma is that last comma in my second example, above. Not everyone believes in it or uses it. I always use it. Compare it to this next sentence, which ignores the Oxford comma:

In the back seat of the car, I found a bag of marijuana, a pack of Marlboros and a vial of pills.

To me, this sentence is less clear. It sounds like the bag of marijuana was somehow separate from the cigarettes and the pills. Do you see my point yet? Let's make it a little more obvious. Compare these sentences:

In the back seat of the car, I found a bag of marijuana, a pack of Marlboros and a vial of pills in a bag.

In the back seat of the car, I found a bag of marijuana, a pack of Marlboros, and a vial of pills in a bag.

Before you weigh in on which sentence you like better, let me post the following question: exactly what was in the bag I found?

The first example lacks precision. Were the cigarettes in the bag with the pills? Sure, as you are writing your report, you know exactly where the cigarettes were. But in six months, or three years, when the case finally goes to trial, and you are refreshing your recollection by reviewing your reports, will that sentence help you?

Compare to the second example. You know exactly what was in the bag. That sentence has precision and clarity. It's the better sentence. The Oxford comma saves the day. Remember, words are important, but so is punctuation.

In Volume 1, I devoted quite a bit of time to punctuation. I think I adequately covered the topic, but just to reiterate, commas, periods, and quotation marks, when used improperly, can completely change the meaning of a sentence. Always proof-read your work.

H. Use of the Possessive

Compare:

The son bears honey.

The sun bear's honey.

Do you know the difference here? In the first sentence, *bears* is a verb. It signifies an action. The second example is singular possessive: the honey belonging to one bear. The third example is plural possessive: the honey belonging to two or more bears. In case you are wondering, a sun bear is a very small, very angry species of bear that can be found in Asia.

Anyway, putting the apostrophe in the wrong place, or forgetting it entirely, can completely change the meaning of a sentence. How would you like to be cross examined for an hour because of an apostrophe? Compare these two sentences:

Based on the evidence, I determined it was the gang member's drugs.

Based on the evidence, I determined it was the gang members' drugs.

In the first example, the drugs belonged to one person. In the second example, the drugs belonged to multiple people.

Precision is important. I talked about precision in Volume 1, and it's subsumed within this entire book. Save yourself hours on the stand under cross examination and make your writing correct, clear, concise, and precise (note the proper use of the Oxford comma).

There's another reason to be correct, clear, concise, and precise. Errors in writing and confusing sentences can distract and will confuse the reader.

Here's another apostrophe example. Let's use the same example of gang members and drugs. Say you arrested two of them.

After arrest, I searched the occupant's bags and found crack pipes.

After arrest, I searched the occupants' bags and found crack pipes.

In case you are still having trouble with this rule, let me explain. The first example refers to a single occupant's bags. The second example indicates you searched the bags of multiple occupants. In addition to not properly identifying the individuals, can you think of anything else wrong?

Do you see the difference? Depending on the actual facts, one or the other example is correct. The first example is pretty clear and probably doesn't need revision. However, the second example has some precision problems. Let's test your understanding. In whose bags were the crack pipes found? If this case goes to trial three years from now, will you remember? Actually, there's a lot wrong with these sentences.

Let's see- (1) How many crack pipes? (2) Which bags? (3) Condition of the pipes? (Did they contain residue? Were they sent for testing?) (4) Where exactly were the bags? (5) What did you do with the bags and evidence? (6) How many occupants, how many bags?

One more thing- never, ever, ever, pluralize a word or abbreviation by adding an apostrophe.

Here's a few examples:

Two DUIs. NOT two DUI's.

Two cops. NOT two cop's.

Two arrests. NOT *two arrest's.*

OK, let's not beat a dead horse.

I. Subject Verb Agreement

I know this rule, and even I sometimes violate it. It's easy to slip up with subject verb agreement, even though it's an easy rule: if the subject of a sentence is singular, the verb must be singular. If the subject is plural, the verb must be plural. Sounds easy, right? Here's an example:

*The worst part of my day **were** when I was dispatched to all those domestics.*

*One of my arrestees **want** to smoke a cigarette before we go to jail.*

Are those mistakes obvious? Compare them to these sentences:

*The worst part of my day **was** when I was dispatched to all those domestics.*

*One of my arrestees **wants** to smoke a cigarette before we go to jail.*

If you understand the parts of a sentence, you can easily check your work. If you break down these sentences to only the subject and verb, it should be obvious.

The worst part was . . .

One of (them) wants. . .

Does that make sense? Let's review a couple more.

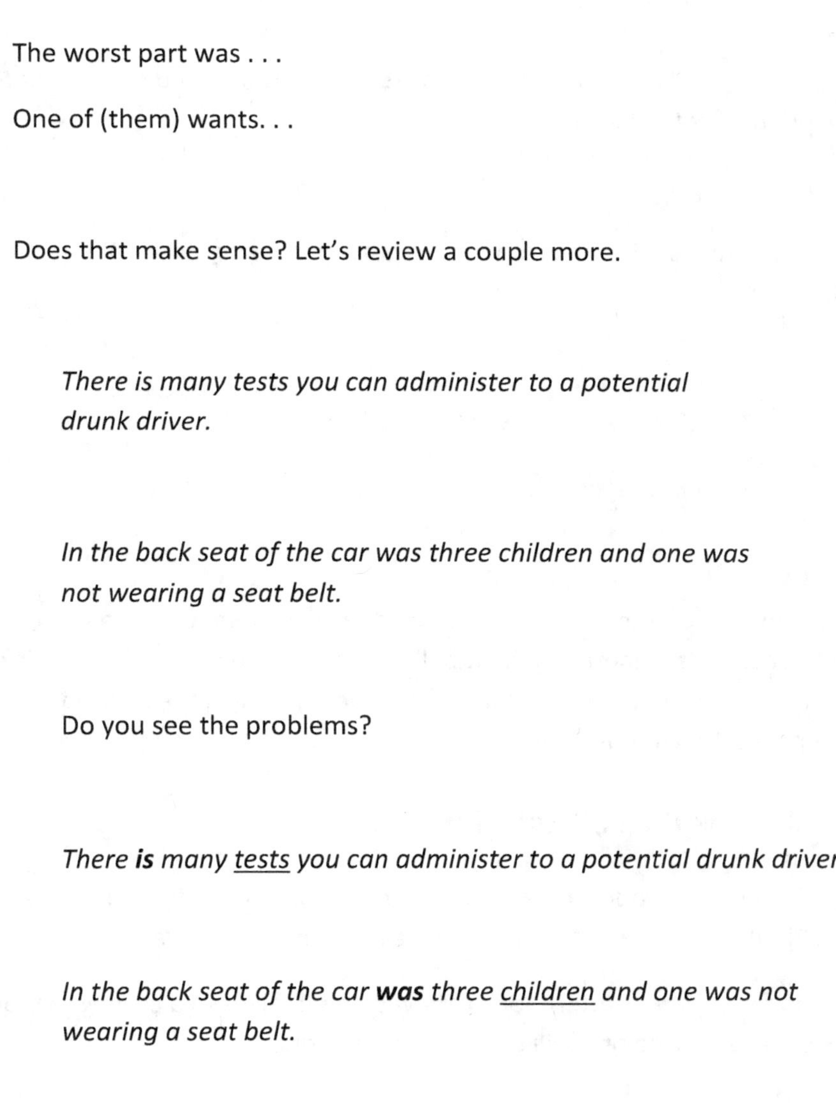

There is many tests you can administer to a potential drunk driver.

In the back seat of the car was three children and one was not wearing a seat belt.

Do you see the problems?

*There **is** many <u>tests</u> you can administer to a potential drunk driver.*

*In the back seat of the car **was** three <u>children</u> and one was not wearing a seat belt.*

The verbs used in these examples are singular, but the subjects, tests and children, are both plural. The correct versions are:

*There **are** many tests you can administer to a potential drunk driver.*

*In the back seat of the car **were** three children and one was not wearing a seat belt.*

Sometimes it is not clear whether a subject is singular or plural. Check this out:

The married couple wants to go home.

The married couple want to go home.

Which is correct? Is "soup and salad" a single item on the menu? What about "spaghetti and meatballs?" "Pork and beans?" I don't think there is a hard and fast rule for this. Personally, I think the first married couple sentence sounds better.

J. Misplaced Modifiers

This is a fun topic. It is also a straightforward and logical rule, and one that is abused and violated in almost every e-mail I receive.

In fact, just this afternoon I received an e-mail from a colleague that exemplifies my point. I will paste it here, unedited:

We will need to discuss that Friday e-mail on the secure system.

As I am writing this sentence, I have no idea which e-mail my colleague is talking about. Is he talking about an e-mail I sent Friday on our secure system? Is he talking about an e-mail sent over some other system, and we need to discuss it over our secure system? Who sent that Friday e-mail? Me? Him?

From what I can tell, this sentence should have been written in one of these formats:

We will need to discuss that Friday e-mail **[I, you, someone else]** *sent on the*

secure system.

We will need to **[get on the secure system]** *and discuss that Friday e-mail* **[I, you, someone else] sent.**

I sent him a reply asking him for some clarification.

Once you are sensitized to this particular issue, you will probably notice it in the majority of the informal communications you receive and send, such as e-mails and text messages. The more you notice it and the more time you waste trying to decipher such messages, the more aware you will be of violating the same rule.

Let's look at another example:

The prisoner was in the cell being monitored by the guard I arrested.

Who did you arrest? The prisoner or the guard? Does this sound better?

The prisoner I arrested was in the cell being monitored by the guard.

Sometimes a misplaced modifier is not only wrong, but downright silly.

I had arrested the prisoner for stealing a silver man's watch.

Have you ever seen a silver man? The modifier, "silver," is misplaced. Try this instead:

I had arrested the prisoner for stealing a man's silver watch.

It's important to proof-read your work to make sure what you wrote is what you meant to write!

I could write twenty pages of great examples of misplaced modifiers:

Just Tom was selected for the officer of the year award. (The officer's name was "Just Tom?")

Try: *Tom was just selected for the officer of the year award.*

I arrested the subject for drunk driving quickly. (I guess the drunk driver was driving fast?)

Try: *I quickly arrested the subject for drunk driving.*

Joe only struggled with the subject for a few minutes before subduing him. (Just Joe? Nobody helped?)

Try: *Joe struggled with the subject for only a few minutes before subduing him.*

I observed the dealer sell the bag to the woman containing methamphetamine. (There's methamphetamine in the woman? Does that mean she had used methamphetamine, or was she smuggling it somewhere? Why was she buying a bag? What was inside?)

Try: *I observed the dealer sell the bag containing methamphetamine to the woman.*

OK, I think you get the picture. Always read your messages before you send them. Misplaced modifiers can confuse the reader and even get you in trouble. Consider the fact some of these informal communications can end up in a defense attorney's hands during discovery in a case.

Part Two

2. Beyond the Basics: Special Topics for Special Situations

Volume 1, and Part One of this volume, give you the basics. In thinking about what else you should have for your tool belt, I'd like to add a few other concepts that are important.

A. Discovery/Multiple Statements (telling the story in multiple documents or multiple ways is bad)

I worked with an investigator who liked to recap his entire investigation with each interview report. Imagine this: his first report was concise and to the point. His second report summarized the first one, then went into the new information. After a three year investigation, his reports were dozens of pages long and only introduced a couple of new sentences. It was virtually impossible to read and understand.

There is a time and place to summarize an investigation: search warrant affidavits, for example, or a summary at the end of your investigation. However, an interview report should be just that and nothing more.

The problem with this investigator's reports was they were unnecessarily repetitive. His rationale was that each report stood on its own. I suppose this was useful in the odd and unlikely case he somehow lost all his prior reporting. By the time the suspects went to jail, he turned a 5,000 word investigation into a 50,000 word case.

In addition to having a long, boring, and confusing narrative, an even bigger problem was that each prior report had to be summarized in fewer and fewer words. A five page interview report taken early in the investigation became a two page report in his subsequent report, and by the end it became a single sentence. Unless you exercise the painstaking care of a micro surgeon, you are bound to have inconsistencies with each new iteration.

Each department and agency will have their own methods for handling this problem. At the police department, we had incident reports and supplemental narrative reports. Nothing else. At the FBI, they have interview reports (FD-302), electronic communications (FD-1057) and many others types of forms. Interviews and anything else testimonial in nature are recorded on the FD-302. Summaries of the investigation can be recorded on ECs.

Multiple statements can be a huge problem when it is time for court. Even the best writers cannot describe something two different ways without some degree of confusion.

> The man's shirt was blue with yellow trim and he was wearing a ball cap.
>
> The man had a hat on, and a blue and yellow shirt.
>
> The man's shirt was blue and yellow, and he wore a hat.

This harkens back to my comments about precision. If you wrote three separate reports and described this man differently in each report, as in the above examples, you might have some difficulties under cross examination.

B. Side Note: Recorded statements

What if you have an audio recording of your interview of a suspect? Your department probably has policies on the recording of interviews. Whatever the case, if you record an interview, the clearest and most accurate documentation would be a transcript. When I recorded an interview of a suspect, my interview report provided the date, the identity of the speakers, the circumstances, and nothing more. Sometimes I included a one or two sentence explanation of the reason for the interview. (Note, your department may have specific policies, so take my words with a grain of salt.)

Whenever you summarize an interview, you are distorting it. It's human nature. It's impossible not to create ambiguity. Thus, it is impossible to accurately summarize a conversation when you have the recording. So here are my recommendations:

1. If you record an interview, then your written report should give only the basics, and perhaps a one sentence summary, for example: "The witness described his observations on the day of the robbery."

2. If you record an interview, make sure you document the circumstances of the recording, who else was there, duration, etc. Of course, if you are interviewing the suspect in a crime, there are many other things you should document, such as the duration of the interview, whether they were told they were free to leave, etc., but that is beyond the scope of this book.

3. If you do not record an interview, and it is an important one, you should have a second officer present to ensure your report is accurate. Both of you should sign off on the final product. This will help eliminate potential ambiguity.

4. Keep your notes. They might clear up any confusion in the future. Keep in mind they will be discoverable. (See **In Your Back Pocket**.)

C. Spell Check is Not Your Friend

I could have titled this section **Sleep With One Eye Open**. Whether you use a word processing program or whatever your department has on-board in your car, one way or another you will be tempted to rely on some kind of spell check program. That's fine, but be very careful. They will look for obviously misspelled words, but not necessarily the correct usage.

Read the following example and identify the three mistakes that spell check might not have caught:

The driver said his breaks stopped working and he crashed in to the udder car.

Now read the correct version:

*The driver said his **brakes** stopped working and he crashed **into** the **other** car.*

In short- trust, but verify.

D. Homophones

What happens when you don't have spell check at all? There are still departments that require some reports to be typed or handwritten. On such occasions, you will be on your own. Even if you have spell checkers, beware of the dreaded homophones! There are hundreds of them, and I won't waste a lot of your time explaining them. Just be aware of them and know the difference.

> There/Their/They're
> Its/It's/Its'
> To/Too/Two
> Wear/Where/Ware
> Cops/Copse

E. Informal and/or Public Communications

OK, I admit it. This section has nothing to do with grammar or official writings. But it's just as important. Please pay attention!

You enjoy the same protections as every other American citizen. The First Amendment gives you the right to express your opinions verbally, in written form, on social media. However, tolerance for law enforcement officers expressing their opinions seems to be at an all-time low.

When people are writing informal communications, whether on social media or in personal e-mails, they tend not to pay as much attention to grammar, spelling, and appropriate content.

There are gratuitous emojis sprinkled in for added flavor. There are ambiguities, slang, abbreviations, inside jokes. That's fine if you are writing a family member, a close friend, but keep one thing in mind: if you are arresting people and making cases against them, at some point there will be a defense attorney trolling through anything about you they can find. Public social media posts are a gold mine for collecting impeachment evidence and cross-examination material. Suddenly, that joke you put on Facebook isn't so funny....

There is no place for racial, gender, or any other bias in law enforcement. If you have such a bias, find another job or get some training or help to overcome it. Don't tolerate it when you see it in your peers. Law enforcement officers are being terminated (or never hired in the first place) with increasing frequency for the content of their social media posts. If you are disciplined for such behavior, it will not be a successful defense to argue you "didn't mean it" or "it was just a joke." In short- don't ruin your career over a silly comment on Facebook.

This book is all about writing, but I feel compelled to point out that sometimes it's best not to write anything. I recently re-posted an article about a police officer that was accidentally shot. The writer of the article suggested the shooter was a protestor at an anti-police rally. Someone took issue with the suggestion that the shooter was a protester, and posted a comment that the article distorted the facts. I responded that I only posted the article to decry violence against the police. This was met with more comments from this person decrying the false narrative that the "non-violent" protesters were involved.

After a few days I re-read our exchange. I said nothing wrong, and nothing that I thought failed the Sixty Minutes test. However, such an exchange might be distorted by a defense attorney one day, or the department with whom I am employed might think the exchange somehow violated some internal policy (it didn't). In any event, I deleted the entire exchange. Sometimes it's best simply not to engage and not to write a response.

F. In Your Back Pocket

I referenced this sub-section within **Atmospherics**. Maybe I should have moved this part closer to that sub-section.

When I was in uniform, the department gave us notepads that fit in our back pockets. Every officer used them differently. I liked to write down each call including the type of call, the dispatch time, arrival time, departure time. When I checked someone for license status, wants/warrants, I wrote down their information. I also took notes that would eventually find their way into a report. Sometimes I was in a hurry and just wrote notes in the corner of a page already filled with ink. Sometimes I wrote on the back cover.

Remember when I said your supervisor might tell you to remove information that wasn't directly relevant to the investigation? Does that mean you cannot record that information? Of course not. Your notepad is where it should go. Anything that might jog your memory of a call can be recorded in that notebook.

Out of curiosity, I conducted a personal exercise: I lined up all my notepads and randomly thumbed through the pages. Some of these notes were taken over 25 years ago. I admit that many, if not most, of my notes were completely foreign to me. But in some of the cases, when I recorded unique, albeit irrelevant facts, it did jog my memory.

The longest time I ever experienced between day of incident and day of testimony was around five years. Under ordinary circumstances, I would have forgotten most of the details of that incident (actually, it was a car crash), but this was a special case. I investigated a car crash where the at-fault driver was an off-duty EMT. The case was pretty straight-forward; he ran a red light and broad-sided another car.

He never informed me he was an EMT, and I issued him a traffic citation and sent him on his way. I probably worked hundreds of accidents just like that one, and but for what followed, I never would have given him a second thought. A few weeks later, at his court date, he appeared in the courthouse in uniform. After chastising him for not telling me at the scene (right or wrong, I did not like to write EMTs tickets because I could be the next cop on their gurney), I approached the solicitor and insisted she drop the ticket.

The solicitor did the best she could. She offered him a plea of guilty with no fine and no points against his license. He took the deal.

Pan forward almost five years. The second driver's insurance company sued the first driver, and the matter went into litigation. I was asked to provide deposition testimony by the lawyer representing the EMT's insurance company. Because of the circumstances surrounding this case, I had a very strong memory of what happened, and I was able to provide testimony with minimal refreshing of my recollection from my notes.

With that said, I make the following recommendations for you:

1. Try to maintain some kind of order to your notepads. Mark the cover with the dates you used the notepad, and when they are full, keep them somewhere safe.

2. Try to keep separate calls/cases on separate pages. Write down the date of each call. Be careful what you write. Remember the Sixty Minutes test: just because they are your personal notes does not mean they are immune from discovery. You might have to provide copies to the prosecutor in the case.

3.   Write whatever you think will help you remember the facts and details. Again, just keep in mind that one day you might have to show those notes to someone else.

4.   Keep them as long as you can. I still have notepads from 1993.

G. E-mails, texts

Does your department assign you an e-mail address? Do you use your personal e-mail for official correspondence? Both are fraught with issues and pitfalls. If you have an official e-mail address, you should always assume it is being monitored and preserved. Your messages (sent and received) can also fall within a discovery request or subpoena. If you are communicating with a confidential source or informant through your e-mail, you should segregate those messages to provide to a prosecutor if that information is related to a case at the discovery phase.

Does that mean you should never use your official e-mail for personal reasons? Most departmental policies allow for *de minimus* use of government facilities like an e-mail address, so if your spouse e-mails you a shopping list so you can stop at the market on your way home, I can't imagine you being disciplined for it. You should realize, however, that your shopping list may be read by someone in your IT department or Internal Affairs, or perhaps due to an overproduction of records through discovery.

So if the general rule is that you should avoid using your work e-mail for personal matters, the corollary is also true: You really should try to avoid using your personal e-mail addresses for work-related matters. When you wrap up an investigation and drive down to the prosecutor's office to hand over all the evidence and investigative reports, the prosecutor will ask you if there are any recorded statements from any witnesses, victims, suspects, in any type of recorded or electronic format. When they ask about witnesses, they mean you, too. That could open up your personal e-mails to inspection. You will have to segregate those messages from all your personal activity.

The fact such messages are on your Hotmail or Yahoo account does not immunize them from discovery. In fact, if you are involved in civil litigation, a court could serve a subpoena and take your e-mails, and then someone would be able to review all your personal messages in order to find those that are responsive to the subpoena. Do you want that to happen?

Part Three

3.   Sworn Statements

A. Affidavits.

OK, let's dive right in.

Writing an affidavit is different from writing an incident report. An incident report is not evidence and generally is not admissible. An affidavit is a sworn statement, made under oath, and is often considered evidence (depending on the court and the state's definition of hearsay).

An affidavit is the written equivalent of you raising your hand and swearing to a judge and providing truthful testimony in a courtroom. You aren't just telling the judge the facts, you are telling the judge who you are, and explaining why the judge should believe you. Your affidavit will also include your personal and professional opinion that there is evidence of a crime in a certain place, or perhaps your opinion about what something is (or isn't).

I am not going to teach you all the mechanics of writing an affidavit. Frankly, I couldn't do that even if I wanted to. The rules are different depending on the type of affidavit and the jurisdiction. Some departments don't even have their officers write their own affidavits, preferring to have the prosecutor write them!

In writing this book, I must assume you have already received some training in writing sworn statements. Many, if not most, of you have already written at least one or two of them in your career. Just like I assume you already generally know how to write an incident report, I will assume you already, generally, know how to write an affidavit.

All the rules are the same. Grammar and punctuation are important. Clarity is important. Giving only truthful facts and opinions are crucial. Everything we have discussed applies to sworn statements, but I want to make a few additional points that specifically apply to these writings.

1. Introductions

Just like your mother might have told you when you were young, first impressions are important. This is where you get to tell the judge about your education, your experience, how long you have been working as a LEO, and whatever else you think helps the judge believe he or she can trust you. It also goes to your credibility. Why should the reader believe you? How many investigations have you conducted like the one about which you are writing? What training, education, and experience have you had that should make the reader respect your opinion?

2. Description of premises

Be specific. Be articulate. Describe the structure. Think about your ancient Uncle that insists on giving you very detailed, very long directions to his house, even though you've been there a hundred times. What color is the mailbox? What kind of roof does it have? You have all read stories about search warrants executed at the wrong residence. People have accidentally been shot and killed because of such mistakes. Maybe you are thinking to yourself that you have been to the place a hundred times. What if you get sick the night before the search and you can't attend? Who will execute the warrant? What if they've never been there before? Take the extra time and give a proper description of the premises. You can never give too much information in this description. What if the subject premises is painted a different color while you are at the courthouse? It happens. Luckily, if you described the premises with enough detail, it won't matter.

Consider also that a defense attorney might one day review the description to determine whether it sufficiently described the premises to be searched. This is an objective test: would a reasonable officer have been able to find the premises with reasonable certainty? It doesn't matter whether you found it or not: it matters whether this fictitious reasonable man would have been able to find it. A judge might suppress all the evidence because you just "got lucky" and hit the right house.

3. Opinions

Facts are king, but opinions are necessary, too. Your opinion whether someone is guilty is irrelevant. Your opinion about whether the evidence in your case provides sufficient probable cause to believe the suspect committed a crime is relevant. Your opinion that evidence of a specific crime will be found at a location is relevant. Your opinion that certain items found at a house are indicative of drug use is relevant. Before signing a search warrant, a judge needs to be convinced that you believe there is probable cause of something.

Pursuant to the Four Corners Rule, a judge will usually only consider what is within your affidavit. If you forget something, you will probably have to edit your affidavit and return. Different judges handle this differently, but as a general rule, you should try to ensure every single relevant fact and opinion is within the four corners of your affidavit. If not, you should point out in your affidavit that you have additional information if what you submitted was not enough.

In some cases, you might be deemed an expert witness. To be declared an expert requires specific procedures that differ between jurisdictions and is beyond the scope of this book.

4. Sourcing/Attribution

If you saw the gun under the couch, then say so. Write it down. If the lady next door told you she saw the gun under the couch, that's what you should put in your affidavit. There is simply no way around it. Whoever found the items is the seizing witness. Whoever saw the gun under the couch is the witness, not the one who wrote about it. We already discussed this earlier when I mentioned keeping a Woods file. But now I want to expand the scope.

HOT TIP: Think outside the box: Don't be afraid to cite newspaper articles or outside studies, even statistics. Right before I was going to execute a search warrant in a case, the prosecutor told me he didn't think there was enough probable cause to believe the main suspect had a computer on the premises. In truth, I didn't know for sure whether he had one. I simply assumed he had one. I did some quick Google research and found a federal government study that listed percentages of Americans who owned a computer. My suspect was a public official with a Masters degree, and this study said a male with an advanced degree in his age group was around 70% likely to own a computer. I cited the source in my affidavit, and it was enough to convince the judge there probably was a computer at his premises.

In Volume 1, I spent an entire chapter on attribution. As a reminder, attribution is the practice of attributing a quoted statement to its speaker. When I say sourcing, I generally am talking about attributing a quoted statement or concept to a written source. This is most applicable to writing affidavits.

In academic writing, or legal writing, every concept should have a source. (Again, remember our earlier discussion about Woods files.)

Bonus Part 1

Knowing When You Can Break the Rules

Rules are rules, right? Well, not really. I worked with another LEO who used to say, when faced with a difficult issue that might involve violating departmental policy, "Is it unconstitutional? Is it illegal? No? Then who cares?" Such an approach might keep you out of jail, but it won't necessarily keep you employed. Contrary to popular belief, rules are not meant to be broken. But sometimes, in very limited cases, you might be able to break certain rules.

As a LEO, this one might be a little tough. When it comes to grammar, there are such limited cases when applying the rules will lead to absurd results. Compare these sentences:

He began to slowly and carefully walk heel to toe.

He failed to successfully complete the heel to toe test.

He agreed to immediately leave the house.

What do these sentences all have in common? They are all technically wrong! Compare them to these sentences:

He began slowly and carefully to walk heel to toe.

He failed successfully to complete the heel to toe test.

He agreed immediately to leave the house.

These are technically correct. The previous sentences violated the rule of the split infinitive. To put it as simply as possible, an infinitive is the form of a verb preceded by "to." A split infinitive is when you put something between the verb and the word "to."

This rule seems to have fallen out of favor over the past few years, as I see split infinitives in formal writing quite often. It quickly is becoming more of a style and clarity rule. When I started policing, possession of marijuana was a misdemeanor offense. When I left, it was legal. I suppose times change, but for our purposes, you should know the rule so you better know when it's acceptable to break it.

In these examples, applying the rule leads to some awkward sentences, doesn't it? Read them again. Does the split infinitive change the meaning of the sentence? Let's revisit the first example:

He began to slowly and carefully walk heel to toe.

He began slowly and carefully to walk heel to toe.

See any difference in meaning? I don't. The incorrect version actually is less awkward, but in this case, I'd go with the second version. If you were in school, you might lose a point or two for submitting the first sentence, but for our purposes, it's ok. Let's look at the second example.

He failed to successfully complete the heel to toe test.

He failed successfully to complete the heel to toe test.

Is the meaning the same in both versions? I think so. But what about readability? In this case, the correct version is actually more awkward. I'd consider using the first version with the split infinitive. Last example.

He agreed to immediately leave the house.

He agreed immediately to leave the house.

This is a great example. In these sentences, the meaning of the sentence actually could be different. The first example is technically incorrect, but much more readable. More importantly, the second (technically correct) example is vague. He immediately agreed, but when will he leave the house? Immediately? Tomorrow? Not until he can sell the house? See the difference?

The best course of action here is to recognize when you are using an infinitive, be aware when you split them, and know when it is appropriate (or necessary) to split them.

Are you a Star Trek fan? Maybe this will help illustrate my point. Compare these two sentences:

To boldly go where no man has gone before!

Boldly to go where no man has gone before!

One is technically wrong and one is technically right. However, the wrong one is one of the most famous science fiction quotes of all time. You decide! Now, the structure of this quote brings to mind another important rule. Actually, I'm thinking of two rules, often violated together:

sentence fragments, and **beginning a sentence with a preposition**. Consider this narrative:

> *He failed to successfully complete the heel to toe test. But he had a doctor's note.*

We already discussed the first sentence. I included it for context. But the second sentence. Is it a complete sentence? Actually, yes, it is. The problem with that sentence is it began with a preposition. Let's look at it again:

> *But he had a doctor's note.*

In my opinion, this is a special case. If you have room in your document, then you should correct this sentence. Try one of these instead:

> *He failed to successfully complete the heel to toe test. However, he had a doctor' note.*

> *He failed to successfully complete the heel to toe test, but he had a doctor's note.*

If you are writing your field sobriety test (FST) results on a form that does not have sufficient room to write it all out correctly, and you choose to begin your sentence with a preposition as in the example, it violate the rule, but like my friend used to say, there are rules, and there are rules. As a supervisor, I wouldn't kick back your report for corrections.

Before we talk about supervisors, I have a pop-quiz for you. Go back a few paragraphs and tell me if you noticed any mistakes. I want you to re-read this paragraph:

*We already discussed the first sentence. I included it for context. **But the second sentence**. Is it a complete sentence? **Actually, yes, it is.** The problem with that sentence is it began with a preposition. Let's look at it again:*

Did you notice those sentence fragments? The first one has no verb, and the second has no subject. Both are fragments and would cost you points on a grammar test. These would be easy to correct:

*We already discussed the first sentence. I included it for context. **However,** take a look at the second sentence. Is it a complete sentence? **Actually, yes, it is a complete sentence.** The problem with that sentence is it began with a preposition. Let's look at it again:*

Correcting those sentences takes a lot more space, doesn't really give much additional information or clarity to the reader, and, frankly, makes it a clunky paragraph. This is a good example of a situation where breaking the rules might be ok.

Bonus Part 2

Law Enforcement Report Writing, Supervisor's Supplement

Maybe you are a sergeant or lieutenant and don't have to write too many reports any more. Maybe you sit at your desk at the end of the shift and approve all your officers' reports. There are lots of management styles, but I'd like to focus on just three of them.

The Pushover

The Pushover Supervisor just approves everything without reading a single page. Maybe this supervisor will glance at a sentence or two just to make sure they are legible, but doesn't read for clarity or content, or anything at all. Officers love this supervisor because they never have to make any corrections, and they can get out the door at the end of their shift quickly and without a hassle.

Later, when those officers have to talk to a detective, testify in court, or answer to some prosecutor before a grand jury hearing, they learn that their original incident report was confusing, vague, ambiguous, inaccurate, or embarrassingly filled with errors. Perhaps ten more minutes in the precinct making corrections would have been less painful than dealing with the consequences of those errors later.

The Grammar Guerilla

On the other extreme is the Grammar Guerilla. The Grammar Guerilla shows up to the precinct with a red pen and a cup of coffee, and gleefully attacks your reports. This supervisor takes personal pleasure in hunting for every single typographical error, every vague sentence, every misspelling. The Grammar Guerilla demands absolute perfection in every report and will settle for nothing less.

Later, when you have to go to court to testify about the case, prosecutors and judges commend your work. Defense attorneys will slam their fists on the table trying to find something about which to cross-examine you. Thanks to all the overtime you earned correcting all your mistakes, you can afford to buy a new truck, but you dread reporting for work each day, knowing the Grammar Guerilla is rubbing his knuckles together and eagerly awaiting your paper.

I wrote that I wanted to discuss three management styles, and that was only two of them. The third is the **Reasonable Supervisor**.

The Reasonable Supervisor recognizes all the mistakes in your reports, but is willing to ignore them unless glaring, or unless they change or confuse the meaning of the sentence. Perhaps this supervisor will let your mistakes slide unless there are too many, in which case you might have to rewrite it. Or maybe this supervisor will review your report, and if there is a serious mistake that must be corrected, then he or she might ask you to correct all the minor problems, too. I was this latter kind of supervisor.

I hold a degree in English Literature and I write a lot. I can see typos from a mile away. Context, syntax, subject/verb agreement, and just about any other kind of problem. (I don't use an editor because I don't trust them. If you find a typo in this book, let me know and I'll send you a free novel I wrote under another name!) After working with my colleagues for many years, I was put in the position of reviewing and approving their work, and I was shocked and disappointed to read some of their reports. So many errors!

The system my department used (we were all electronic) did not allow me to make any corrections to someone else's work; otherwise, I at least would have handled the minor typos myself. In the alternative, I could have printed the reports then corrected them by hand and returned them to my officers, but that went against the entire purpose for "going paperless." So what was I to do?

I read each report, reviewed the errors, and if they were serious enough, or numerous, I would return them for corrections. The first time, I would try to be helpful by pointing out the errors, in the hopes I would encounter the same ones only infrequently. Most of them made the corrections, and they rarely repeated them. A small handful, however, continued to make the same mistakes, and after a few attempts to explain the errors, I just kicked the reports back without comment. Those few officers really struggled. They were not good writers, but it was my job to make sure the final product reflected positively on our department, and as their supervisor, it was also my job to protect them from embarrassment, and protect the integrity of the cases they had investigated.

In order to evaluate someone's written product, you also must be cognizant of the rules. You may no longer be writing reports, but it is now even more important for you to know the rules and guide your officers. Rubber stamping their work will eventually hurt them, hurt their cases, and hurt you and your department. An occasional missed comma won't cause too much damage, but if you have enough of them, you might have a problem. Be fair, be reasonable, but take a hard look at every report before you approve it. Lives may hang in the balance!

Getting Past Police Work- Personnel Matters

If you work for the government, you will get at least an annual review, also known as a performance appraisal, yearly evaluation, or whatever else your department calls it. If you are a supervisor, you will most likely be writing one of these documents.

All the same rules that you encountered in these books apply to these reviews. Following all those rules are a necessary, but not sufficient, requirement to writing a proper review. Because this book is about professional writing and not just grammar, I would like to offer a few suggestions.

Be Specific

Let's say an officer, Joe, was dispatched to a domestic. Another officer, Mary, hearing the dispatch and knowing she was close to the call, announced on the radio that she would assist. Mary arrived first, waited for the dispatched officer, and together they made contact with the victim. The suspect was in the back yard. After collecting the victim's statement, the officers went into the back yard to confront the suspect. A fight ensued, during which the officers tried to subdue the man. Mary pinned the suspect to the ground so that Joe could handcuff him.

Sound like good work, right? Although beyond the scope of this book, as a supervisor you might want to jot down some notes about that incident. Perhaps you should save a copy of the report in their personnel file.

When it is time for the officers' annual reviews, a good supervisor will use concrete and specific examples of the officers' work to demonstrate their competence (or lack thereof). Using the example above, the supervisor should be specific, then explain why the facts are demonstrative of that officer's performance during the reporting period. Let me break down the paragraph above into the main facts and show you what I mean:

Joe was dispatched to a domestic.

Mary, hearing the dispatch and knowing she was close to the call, announced on the radio that she would assist.

Mary arrived first.

Mary waited for the dispatched officer, and together they made contact with the victim.

After collecting the victim's statement, the officers went into the back yard to confront the suspect.

A fight ensued, during which the officers tried to subdue the man.

Mary pinned the suspect to the ground so that Joe could handcuff him.

Let's talk about Mary. If you are her supervisor and writing her review, this is a great example to cite. Each fact I separated is demonstrative of some behavior. Let me show you what I mean:

Mary, hearing the dispatch and knowing she was close to the call,   announced on the radio that she would assist.

Mary exercised excellent initiative by proactively assisting Joe.

Mary arrived first.

Mary recognized the importance of the call and did not dawdle.

Mary waited for the dispatched officer, and together they made contact with the victim.

Mary exercised excellent officer safety by waiting for back up to arrive.

Mary pinned the suspect to the ground so that Joe could handcuff him.

Mary exercised excellent teamwork and courage by pinning down the suspect so her partner could handcuff him.

The two parts here are, first, documenting specific behavior that is demonstrative of the employee's performance, and, second, an explanation of why the behavior is notable.

Such a narrative will be helpful for a performing employee; perhaps the narrative could be used in submitting her name for an award, or to help her compete for a promotion. But, as any supervisor would agree, not all employees are like Mary. Let's look at a different scenario, this time using another officer who we will call Bad Mary.

> *Bad Mary was dispatched to a domestic. Another officer, Joe, hearing the dispatch, announced on the radio that he would assist even though he was far away. Joe arrived first, waited for the dispatched officer, and together they made contact with the victim. The suspect was in the back yard. After collecting the victim's statement, the officers went into the back yard to confront the suspect. A fight ensued, during which Joe tried to subdue the man while Mary watched. Eventually Joe was able to handcuff the suspect.*

Big difference, right? Let's break down this paragraph and provide some constructive criticism.

> *Bad Mary was dispatched to a domestic. Another officer, Joe, hearing the dispatch, announced on the radio that he would assist even though he was far away. Joe arrived first.*

Despite being closer to the scene of the domestic, Bad Mary arrived after her backup officer. Bad Mary is encouraged and expected to respond expeditiously to dispatches.

A fight ensued, during which Joe tried to subdue the man while Bad Mary watched. Eventually Joe was able to handcuff the suspect.

Bad Mary is expected to support her colleagues when they need help. Bad Mary should have assisted Joe in subduing the suspect.

This is obviously a sterile example that does not consider mitigating factors (perhaps Bad Mary got stuck in traffic or got lost), and does not discuss corrective action, as both are very fact sensitive and will depend in large part on the department and department policy, work history of the employee, and many other factors. The main point of this section is to illustrate that a supervisor should be descriptive in their reviews of their employees, and document how the descriptions of behavior demonstrate the employee's level of performance.

Summary

I hope you found this brief grammar discussion helpful. As you can see, there are a lot of rules you have to keep in mind when you are writing for your profession. Those rules exist (and most are absolute necessities) to make sure your readers understand what you are trying to say. Putting a comma in the wrong place can completely change the meaning of a sentence. Putting a clause in the wrong part of a sentence can also destroy the meaning.

Remember: clarity is king. The rules I have discussed in Volume 1 and Volume 2 exist to make sure your writing means what you intend. But, perhaps more important than the rules themselves, is the goal of clarity. That means there will be times when a grammar rule should be ignored.

There is another reason why there may be times when the rules can be bent or even broken. The strict application of grammar rules can lead to stilted sentences, stuffy paragraphs, and imbue you, the writer, with the tone of a stiff, old English teacher. So after writing two books all about grammar and how to write, I am adding, in these final paragraphs, the freedom to ignore some of the rules when it satisfies the greater purpose- making sure the meaning you intend is the meaning you write.

Just as a reminder, if you enjoyed this book, please write an honest review on Amazon and/or all the usual places. Once it's published, e-mail me at stevenstarklight@yahoo.com and paste the review. As a way of saying thank you, I will send you an electronic copy of Grammar Saves Lives, Volume 1, for free!

I wish you all the best- a long, meaningful, and safe and healthy career and life.

Other Books to Read from Overkill Press:

by Steven Starklight

How to Become a Police Officer: The Best Tactics to Get Police Officer Jobs and enter the Police Academy

Grammar Saves Lives, Volume 1

Golem

By Jonathan B. Zeitlin

Death and Repair; a Michael Hart Mystery

The Body in the Hole; The Undertaker Series, Book 1

The Body in the Bed; The Undertaker Series, Book 2